KANT'S
PRINCIPLE OF
PERSONALITY

Hardy E. Jones

KANT'S PRINCIPLE OF PERSONALITY

The University of
Wisconsin Press
Madison, Milwaukee,
and London

Published 1971
The University of Wisconsin Press
Box 1379, Madison, Wisconsin 53701

The University of Wisconsin Press, Ltd.
70 Great Russell Street, London, WC1B 3BY

First printing

Printed in the United States of America
Impressions, Inc., Madison, Wisconsin

ISBN 0-299-06020-9; LC 70-157393

For Judith

CONTENTS

PREFACE

This book is an interpretation and critique of Kant's principle that human beings ought to be treated as ends-in-themselves, never merely as means. It has been written with the hope of increasing our present understanding of Kant's moral philosophy. The doctrine examined herein is reflected in much popular talk of "de-humanization," "human dignity," and "treating persons as things." I have attempted a philosophical analysis of the principle as it is understood and employed by one of the very few great thinkers about morality. In my judgment, this formulation of the categorical imperative has been slighted in most books on Kant. My aim has been to diminish this deficiency with a systematic, thorough account of the principle as it relates to the larger structure of Kant's ethical theory and to fundamental moral beliefs.

It will be obvious that I am quite sympathetic with Kant's emphasis on the moral importance of human beings as ends-in-themselves in possession of absolute value. But I have also tried to be attentive to the serious and deep difficulties of explicating and justifying principles based on these lofty sentiments. I have not hesitated to indicate where and why I believe Kant to be mistaken. The account of these weaknesses has the constructive purpose of pointing toward a sounder theory. I have restrained myself from including too many of my own ideas for a Kant-inspired (if not Kantian) re-interpretation and justification of the principle of personality.

The book is a revision of my doctoral thesis presented at the University of Wisconsin in the spring of 1970. I wish to thank several persons whose interest and evaluation have helped to make the work less burdensome and more satisfying than it otherwise might have been. I owe a considerable debt of gratitude to

ix

Marcus G. Singer for his numerous suggestions for improvement. In supervising my work at Wisconsin and in several other ways, he taught me much about Kant and about the methods of philosophical inquiry. Particularly helpful has been Professor Singer's talent for judiciously combining tough criticism and generous encouragement. The other members of the Philosophy Department at Wisconsin have contributed much, directly and indirectly, to the completion of this study. To those who read portions of various versions of the manuscript I am especially indebted. Gerald C. MacCallum commented most conscientiously on some very rough accounts of my first thoughts on the topic. I am grateful also for the comments and criticisms of Claudia Card, Joseph Chassler, and Keith Yandell. A. Phillips Griffiths of the University of Warwick made many helpful suggestions during his year as Visiting Professor at the University of Wisconsin.

My colleagues at the University of Texas have provided me with much stimulation during the preparation of the manuscript. Norman Gillespie in particular has allowed me to test my ideas against his judgment in a series of conversations. During this time I have also benefited greatly from several talks with Keith Lovin of Southwest Texas State University. Other persons who commented on important sections of the manuscript are Donald Affeldt, Gary Baran, William Bortz, and Don Siewert.

It is a pleasure to express feelings of gratitude to my teachers at Baylor University in whose courses I first became interested in the philosophy of Kant. I am most grateful also to Stephen Rosenbaum for his kind remarks on the manuscript and for many years of stimulating personal and philosophical friendship.

The greatest debt of all I owe to my wife, Judith.

HARDY E. JONES

Austin, Texas
July 8, 1971

KANT'S
PRINCIPLE OF
PERSONALITY

ABBREVIATIONS

Throughout this study I have abbreviated the titles of three of Kant's works.

CPR *Critique of Practical Reason.* Translated by Lewis White Beck. Indianapolis: Bobbs-Merrill, 1956.

DV *The Doctrine of Virtue.* Part II of *The Metaphysics of Morals.* Translated by Mary J. Gregor. New York: Harper & Row, 1964.

GW *Groundwork of the Metaphysics of Morals.* Translated by H. J. Paton. New York: Harper & Row, 1964.

INTRODUCTION

Immanuel Kant's *Groundwork of the Metaphysics of Morals* is a rich source of both moral insight and moral perplexity. His famous dictum concerning human dignity—the second formulation of the categorical imperative—is widely regarded as one of the most significant of his insights. He refers to it as the principle of humanity: "Act in such a way that you always treat humanity, whether in your own person or in the person of any other, never simply as a means, but always at the same time as an end" (*GW* 96).

Many readers will perhaps insist that this remark does not provide much insight. But most would surely, upon some reflection, find it perplexing. The practice of slavery has often been declared wrong because it involves the treatment of persons merely as a means. The principle has also been used to condemn a bewildering array of other actions and practices. Among these are punishment, conscription, lying, and suicide. With regard to these and many other cases it is not clear how the formula is to be understood and applied. Though Kant evidently believed it to be very important, he devoted a surprisingly small amount of space to its analysis and application. Partly as a consequence of the sparse character of his discussion, the principle has very often been quite badly misunderstood. Another factor which has led to considerable confusion is its evident emotional appeal. In many discussions of moral problems, one finds it treated as little more than a platitude. And it is often reduced to the status of a mere slogan.

What is needed is a sustained examination of the principle within the context of Kant's whole ethical theory. Kant's second formula can be understood and explained only when one grasps its relation to certain central doctrines of his moral philosophy.

3

Its full importance as a formulation of the categorical imperative can be appreciated only in relation to his claims about objective ends, absolute value, rationality, the will, autonomy, and respect. Acceptance or rejection of Kant's principle may be appropriate, but no one can reasonably do either without understanding it. The main objective of this book is to analyze and clarify it on its own terms and within the philosophical framework from which it is derived.

This is not to say, of course, that a reinterpretation of the principle is unnecessary. Indeed, one of the major conclusions of this book is that revision and elaboration are essential if the principle is to provide practical moral guidance. Thus it becomes important to distinguish clearly between what Kant meant by this second formula of the categorical imperative and what others have interpreted it to mean. Suggestions for reinterpretation will be made throughout the study. But even these ideas have affinities with some of what Kant says and with much of that which underlies his claims about man as an end-in-himself.

The basic idea behind Kant's principle is that human beings have absolute worth. I will attempt an analysis of this notion, which is to some extent independent of Kant's claims in the main texts. Another idea suggested in Kant's formula is that human beings are deserving of respect from their fellows. In this regard the relevance of certain attitudes, motives, and other "internal" phenomena (as opposed to physical actions conceived as "external" events) will be examined. This examination will also be conducted somewhat independently of Kant's central claims. The points developed along these lines become useful in criticism of Kant's own account of the principle.

Some points will also be made about the standard uses of such crucial expressions as "end," "means," and "sharing ends." An effort will be made to compare these meanings with (and where necessary, to differentiate them from) Kant's employment of the same terms. This is an important part of the central task of trying to understand Kant's views. The consideration of certain alternative interpretations of the principle (as well as of different ways of understanding its key terms) will facilitate, through the provision of instructive contrasts, a deeper understanding of his position.

The questions with which I shall deal are mainly questions about the moral philosophy of Kant. But the ways of dealing with them are not restricted to a mere delineation of the intricacies of his thought. Some of this is essential if his views are to be properly understood. The problems on which he focused, however, were not simply issues to be accommodated for the purpose of filling out an ethical system. They are serious matters suggestive of moral dilemmas and provocative of reflection for almost anyone concerned with performing right actions and understanding why they are right. Many of the questions discussed will be of interest and importance to laymen as well as to moral philosophers.

A preliminary account of the main issues may serve to introduce the reader to the central claims to be established. The following questions about the principle of personality have puzzled many: Why are we told that we must treat man as an "end"? What does this mean? If Kant was simply urging respect for human dignity, why was it essential to speak of man as an end-in-himself? These questions are, in my judgment, entirely justified and deserving of answers. I shall be occupied with them directly in the earlier chapters; but from an overall perspective, the entire book may be viewed as an attempt to answer them.

Kant's primary reason for introducing the concept of humanity as an end-in-itself is to provide what he calls the "matter," or "content," for the moral law. Early in the second chapter of the *Groundwork,* he sets forth the first formulation of the categorical imperative: "Act only on that maxim through which you can at the same time will that it should become a universal law" (*GW* 88). This principle, in his view, provides the "form" for morality. Believing it to be exceedingly important and treating it as an essential foundation stone of his moral theory, Kant nevertheless considered it to be insufficient. What was needed was a supplementary principle stating the content for morality. Having furnished the form for the rational will, he thought it necessary to establish an "object" for human volition. In subsequent chapters I shall try to show why Kant believed that man alone could serve as this end.

It is important to note that Kant is in quest of what he calls an "objective end" for the moral law. One of my main contentions is that this notion is ambiguous within the relevant texts, for Kant actually has at least two different conceptions of man as an end. This point is significantly related to the examination of several of Kant's arguments for the view that man is an end-in-himself. My analysis of these arguments rests in part on suggestions concerning which concept of man's status is at issue.

The differences between these two conceptions may be briefly indicated through further attention to questions provoked by Kant's statement of the principle. One might ask: Is Kant claiming that it is always wrong to treat another as a means? Or is he saying that although one does not necessarily act wrongly if he treats someone as a means, his action is condemnable if he treats someone *merely* as a means? If so, what is the difference between treating someone as a means and treating him as a mere means?

These questions, like the ones noted earlier, pose problems with which any detailed account of Kant's principle ought to deal. The remaining chapters show why it is important to consider them and suggest Kantian solutions to them. I shall also try to show why these solutions are inadequate. The difficulties are, broadly, of three sorts: (1) the answers are inadequate to Kant's purpose in introducing the principle, (2) his account is not very helpful in providing moral guidance in cases in which the application of the formula is problematic, and (3) his view has some surprising and unfortunate utilitarian overtones.

In describing actions of treating people as mere means, Kant sets forth what may be termed his negative concept of man as an end. On the basis of this conception, man is not an "end" in any usual or ordinary sense in which the term is used. He is not an end which can be the goal or aim of an action; he is not an end which may be properly thought of as something sought or attained. Man must serve, Kant believes, as the "supreme limiting condition" for all human action and for the attainment of all human ends. Man himself is thus called the end-in-itself. I shall attempt to demonstrate both the plausibility and the limitations of this idea.

This negative conception of man as an end bears an important relationship to another notion absolutely essential to an understanding of Kant's principle—the idea of sharing in an end. In the course of elaborating and applying his principle, Kant condemns actions which "use the person of others merely as a means without taking into consideration that, as rational beings, they ought always at the same time to be rated as ends—that is, only as beings who must themselves be able to share in the end of the very same action" (*GW* 97). This statement may quite understandably raise a new set of questions in the mind of someone unacquainted with Kant's ethical thought. What does Kant mean by "sharing in the ends" of actions? Is the notion of sharing ends the key to the contrast between treating persons as means and treating them as mere means? If so, does the fact that someone shares in the ends for which he is used make the action of treating him as a means morally acceptable?

The problems suggested by these questions are also perfectly legitimate and deserving of attention. I shall try to show that an adequate analysis of Kant's idea of sharing in ends is essential to an understanding of what he means by man as the end-in-itself. Another main contention is that, given what he means by treating persons as ends in the negative way, he does not provide the content or matter for the moral law. Indeed, with the second formula Kant offers very little beyond what he says about the first formulation of the categorical imperative, the principle of universality. Thus I shall argue that Kant does not actually achieve his purpose for setting out the principle of personality.

With the positive conception of man as an end, Kant introduces a totally different set of ideas. These may be outlined with reference to another group of questions about the principle. Is there a way in which humanity may be plausibly thought of as the purpose or goal of actions? What does it mean for man to be sought or attained? Can man be an end in the way in which health or welfare may be the ends of actions? In dealing with these questions, I shall again rely on the distinction between two kinds of objective ends. The sense of "objective end" relevant to Kant's positive conception is that of an end which all persons ought to have.

In *The Doctrine of Virtue* Kant describes two "ends which also are duties": one's own perfection and the happiness of others. These duties are constitutive of one's general duty to treat man as an end in the positive sense (*DV* 44–54). A key to the interpretation proposed is that the obligations to seek happiness and perfection can be understood as duties to realize or advance human nature. One treats man or humanity as an end (in the positive sense) by treating human nature as the goal of one's actions.

Two central contentions emerge from the development of this theme: (1) these notions of perfection and happiness enable Kant to supply objects for human volition and some of the content for the moral law, but (2) with this more positive conception he does not have a way of distinguishing between the treatment of persons as means and the treatment of them merely as means. The emphasis on happiness also provides a more striking indication of the utilitarian aspects of Kant's doctrine of the end-in-itself.

These points of analysis and criticism suggest a further group of questions. In what way do these different conceptions of man as an end-in-himself relate to the notion of human beings' having value? Just why does Kant hold that human beings have absolute worth? Why does he believe that persons have a value which is not limited to their usefulness as means? In attempting to answer these questions I have tried to work out a coherent interpretation of several elements in Kant's theory of value. The emphasis on this feature of Kant's view provides a useful way of demonstrating those respects in which it is contrary to certain versions of utilitarianism. An attempt will be made to indicate how this concept of absolute value—rather than that of sharing in ends—makes Kant's principle of personality attractive and illuminating. But a satisfactory account of these merits and defects cannot be given until we have considered more fully Kant's conceptions of man as an end. A major part of the first chapter is devoted to this task.

1 PERSONS AS ENDS-IN-THEMSELVES

The few paragraphs preceding Kant's introduction of the principle of personality form one of the most puzzling stretches of argument in the *Groundwork of the Metaphysics of Morals*. In this chapter I intend to supply a basis for subsequent discussion by considering his initial claims about humanity as an end-in-itself. It is first essential to note the importance of Kant's view of human nature as both rational and sensible (or sensuous). As a rational agent man has affinities with God as well as with all other rational beings (if any such there be). Man is not a rational being in the sense of being completely or necessarily rational in his actions and thoughts. He is called rational because he can make use of reason and because he has the capacity for making rational decisions in accordance with the requirements of morality. Another feature related to man's rationality is his autonomy. In Kant's view, men are free beings who are subject to the moral law. In order to be free, persons can be subject only to laws of their own creation (*DV* 22; *CPR* 89–90). Thus man is also regarded as a rational being because he is the source or creator of moral laws which must themselves be rational.

Despite its overwhelming importance rationality is only one component in the nature of man. Though man is the source of the moral law and is capable of acting rationally, he does not always do what is right. His actions do not always measure up to that from which moral rules are derived and to that of which he is capable. The reason for this is that man is also a natural and sensible being: he possesses inclinations or desires. In this

9

respect he has affinities with other animals. The inclinations are a constant source of temptation; they continually threaten the making of rational choices in accordance with moral demands. Both rationality and sensibility are absolutely essential to man's nature as a moral agent. Without rationality he could not be capable of morality and could not be held responsible for actions. (Indeed, it is questionable whether he could be properly regarded as performing "actions.") But sensibility is also essential to man's possession of duties. For if he were necessarily and only a rational being, he would be a perfect one. Man's status in regard to the moral law is different from that of God. God is a wholly rational being and one who, of necessity, always acts rationally. It does not make sense to claim that God *ought* to act in accordance with the moral law, for one can be under no duty to act as he would necessarily act. The notions of being subject to the moral law and of having duties presuppose, in Kant's view, the possibility of choosing not to act in accordance with morality. And the possession of desires which often steer man away from virtuous action insures that this is a genuine possibility.

Kant's views on human nature bear an important relationship to his distinction between hypothetical and categorical imperatives. Categorical imperatives are unconditional ones. They are universal principles valid for all rational beings. Hypothetical imperatives, however, are conditional. They depend upon some prior wish or desire. Kant says that "all *imperatives* command either *hypothetically* or *categorically*. Hypothetical imperatives declare a possible action to be practically necessary as a means to the attainment of something else that one wills (or that one may will). A categorical imperative would be one which represented an action as objectively necessary in itself apart from its relation to a further end" (*GW* 82). A hypothetical imperative is thus valid for someone only if he possesses a certain end. A categorical one, however, commands that an action be performed irrespective of whatever ends a person may in fact have.

Morality, in Kant's view, is essentially concerned only with categorical imperatives. The following passage is most instructive:

Finally, there is an imperative which, without being based on, and conditioned by, any further purpose to be attained by a certain line of conduct, enjoins this conduct immediately. This imperative is *categorical*. It is concerned, not with the matter of the action and its presumed results, but with its form and with the principle from which it follows; and what is essentially good in the action consists in the mental disposition, let the consequences be what they may. This imperative may be called the imperative of *morality*. (*GW* 83–84)

What is of special interest in this passage is Kant's remark that a categorical imperative is unconcerned with the matter of an action. The end or "presumed results" are not of importance. What is essential, rather, is the *form* of the action. The form of a morally right action consists in its universality (*GW* 103–4). In accordance with this formal requirement, Kant provides the first formulation of the categorical imperative: "Act only on that maxim through which you can at the same time will that it should become a universal law" (*GW* 88). This formula is often taken to be the most important of Kant's claims about morality. There can be no serious doubt about its crucial role in his ethical theory. Yet Kant apparently came to believe it insufficient for an adequate understanding of morality and the categorical imperative. In the light of the earlier point that a categorical imperative is unconcerned with the matter, one might reasonably conclude that an understanding of the form of moral action is sufficient. In the passages with which we are mainly concerned in this chapter, however, Kant begins to emphasize the matter or end for morality. Indeed he thinks that if some objective end cannot be found, there can be no supreme moral principle and thus no categorical imperative (*GW* 96).

If some sort of end is essential to the existence of a supreme moral principle, how, then, can Kant distinguish between hypothetical and categorical imperatives? Kant's new way of making this distinction is in terms of the kinds of ends which can be the objects of the respective kinds of imperative. Subjective ends can establish only hypothetical imperatives; objective ends are required for categorical ones:

Hence the difference between subjective ends, which are based on impulsions, and objective ends, which depend on motives valid for every rational being. . . . Ends that a rational being adopts arbitrarily as *effects* of his action (material ends) are in every case only relative; for it is solely their relation to special characteristics in the subject's power of appetition which gives them their value. Hence this value can provide no universal principles, no principles valid and necessary for every volition—that is, no practical laws. Consequently all these relative ends can be the ground only of hypothetical imperatives.

Suppose, however, there were something *whose existence* has *in itself* an absolute value, something which as *an end in itself* could be a ground of determinate laws; then in it, and in it alone, would there be the ground of a possible categorical imperative—that is, of a practical law. (*GW 95*)

The distinction between subjective and objective ends is crucial to a sound account of Kant's second formula of the categorical imperative. A general discussion of this distinction is necessary in order to evaluate his initial argument for the claim that man alone is an end-in-itself. There are in the relevant texts actually two characterizations of objective ends, and the distinction between subjective and objective ends is therefore a double one. There is, however, one general feature which applies to objective ends in both senses of the term: they are "equally valid for all rational beings" (*GW 95*). All actions are to be evaluated in terms of this general characterization of objective ends. Such ends are not dependent upon any particular circumstances or desires which may be applicable only to some rational agents.

The first of the two kinds of objective ends is essentially negative. In this sense they are what Kant calls "self-existent." These ends are not produced by human action: they cannot be effects or results. Instead they serve as "supreme limiting conditions." Consider the following passages:

. . . in it [the principle of humanity] humanity is conceived, not as an end of man (subjectively)—that is, as an object which, as a matter of fact, happens to be made an end—but as an objective end —one which, be our ends what they may, must, as a law, constitute the supreme limiting condition of all subjective ends and so must spring from pure reason. (*GW* 98)

Rational nature separates itself out from all other things by the fact that it sets itself an end. An end would thus be the matter of every good will. But in the Idea of a will which is absolutely good— good without any qualifying condition (namely, that it should attain this or that end)—there must be complete abstraction from every end that has to be *produced* (as something which would make every will only relatively good). Hence the end must here be conceived, not as an end to be produced, *but as a self-existent* end. (*GW* 105)

On the basis of these remarks, we may formulate a notion of subjective ends which corresponds to the negative conception of objective ones. Subjective ends would be those which can be the ends or purposes of actions. This use of the term 'end' is consistent with our usual way of understanding it. In this sense ends are the aims and goals of persons and can be thought of as the intended results or effects of what is to be done. (To use Kant's word, they can be 'produced'.) An objective end, however, is "already existent": it is not the sort of thing that one seeks to achieve. Since human beings are already existent and are not produced, it seems quite natural for Kant to speak of them as objective ends.

Kant's resistance to providing ends for the moral law can be seen in his development of this concept. The ends he provides are of a most peculiar sort, quite unlike those which would have been expected. For "self-existent" ends are not really ends at all in any generally accepted sense of the term. Kant thus tends to restrict himself to the form of moral action. Under the guise of the matter he has introduced something which seems wholly inappropriate as an end for the categorical imperative. With this negative conception of ends, Kant has not provided the matter, or content, for the moral law. He tells us little more than is offered with the principle of universality. We are thus left with almost no guidance in determining those cases in which persons are treated as a mere means (as a means to ends in which they cannot share).

There is another sense of "objective ends" which must be

distinguished from this basically negative conception.[1] Consider the following sentence from the *Metaphysics of Morals:* "Only the concept of an obligatory *end,* a concept that belongs exclusively to ethics, establishes a law for the maxims of actions by subordinating the subjective end (which everyone has) to the objective end (which everyone ought to adopt as his own)" (*DV* 48). Here we have a totally different notion, which may conveniently be labeled the positive conception of objective ends. In this sense, objective ends—sometimes referred to by Kant as "ends which also are duties"—are ends which ought to be the aims of everyone's action. According to this positive conception, objective ends would be a subset of the class of subjective ones defined according to the negative conception.

Corresponding to these positive objective ends are subjective ones of a different kind. The latter are characterized as those which people do in fact seek. This second distinction between subjective and objective ends is analogous to Kant's distinction between subjective and objective principles. A subjective principle or maxim is that which one does in fact adopt and act upon, a principle actually made operative by the will. Objective principles are those which a person ought to accept and obey. As a sensible being subject to inclinations and thus not wholly virtuous, he does not by nature act upon them. One who wishes to act morally must bring his subjective principles into line with objective ones. His maxims, then, should be objective principles (or, at the least, compatible with them).

A brief account of Kant's views on happiness may serve to clarify further the two kinds of objective ends and the consequent distinctions between subjective and objective ones. He holds that the happiness of others is an end which every human being ought to adopt (*DV* 53–54). In the positive sense, the happiness of others is an objective end. In the negative sense, however, happiness is only a subjective end, since it may be produced as the result of actions. Kant also holds that each man by nature seeks

---

1. Kant sometimes suggests that the negative interpretation is the only viable conception of the end-in-itself: "It must therefore be conceived only negatively—that is, as an end against which we should never act" (*GW* 105).

his own happiness (*GW* 98). One's own happiness is thus a subjective end in both senses. It is obviously not an objective one in the negative sense. And it cannot be objective in the positive sense because one cannot have a duty to seek that which he necessarily (as a natural being) pursues.

These two characterizations of objective ends provide the basis for two different conceptions of man as an end-in-himself. Humanity is an end in the merely negative sense of a supreme limiting condition restricting the adoption of (subjective) ends and the use of means. But man is also an end in the positive sense: he should be "sought" or "realized" through the development of distinctively human qualities. Despite the fact that Kant sometimes appears to rule out the latter characterization, each of these conceptions forms a major part of his doctrine of the end-in-itself.

ABSOLUTE VALUE AND THE END-IN-ITSELF

These conceptions of objective ends may now be related to Kant's initial arguments for the view that man is an end-in-himself. Kant's first argument is based upon certain elements in his theory of value as well as upon his theory of human nature. After claiming that only something *"whose existence has in itself* an absolute value" can be the ground of a categorical imperative, Kant provides his first statement of the principle of humanity: "Now I say that man, and in general every rational being, *exists* as an end in himself, *not merely as a means* for arbitrary use by this or that will: he must in all his actions, whether they are directed to himself or to other rational beings, always be viewed *at the same time as an end"* (*GW* 95).

Before proceeding to a consideration of Kant's subsequent argument, it is of importance to consider the conception of objective ends which underlies it. In this statement man is an end only in the negative sense. This claim can be supported with reference to Kant's theory of human nature. Kant says in this passage that all rational beings are ends-in-themselves. But not every rational being can be an end in the positive sense. To treat a being as an end in that sense is to seek to develop his moral character and to advance his happiness. God is a rational being, but the notions of perfection and happiness do not apply in his case. Perfection for God cannot be rationally sought, since it is a necessary feature of his being; his happiness cannot be a rational end, since happiness is essentially connected with the satisfaction of inclinations, or sensible desires. In short, the concept of man as an end in the positive sense is partially dependent upon claims about the sensible side of man's nature. As the statement quoted above indicates, however, Kant wishes (at this stage of the discussion) to make man's status as an end-in-himself rest on his rationality alone. He can thus say that every rational being is an end-in-himself.

In order to demonstrate that man is the end-in-itself, Kant makes the following claims: "All the objects of inclination have only a conditioned value; for if there were not these inclinations and the needs grounded on them, their object would be valueless. Inclinations themselves, as sources of needs, are so far from having an absolute value to make them desirable for their own sake that it must rather be the universal wish of every rational being to be wholly free from them. Thus the value of all objects that can *be produced* by our action is always conditioned" (*GW* 95–96). He then describes persons as ends (in the sense of limiting conditions) and says that if they are not self-existent ends, "nothing at all of *absolute* value would be found anywhere. But if all value were conditioned—that is, contingent—then no supreme principle could be found for reason at all" (*GW* 96). The argument may be summarized as follows: In order for there to be a categorical imperative, something must have absolute value. If persons do not have this sort of value, nothing of such value could be found anywhere. Therefore persons must be considered to possess unconditioned worth. For one could not rationally deny this and still claim that there are categorical imperatives.

In speaking of the objects of inclination as having conditioned value, Kant means that whatever value they may have is dependent upon some desire. They are not objectively valuable, since their worth is conditional upon someone's valuing them and upon their being valued for the satisfaction of desires. A troublesome feature of the claim is the ambiguity of the phrase "objects of inclination." In other sections of the *Groundwork* Kant clearly recognizes that a single object may be sought on the basis of both inclination and reason. One may seek a morally worthwhile end both because he desires it (as a sensible being) and because he recognizes the rightness of pursuing it (as a rational being). One of these ends is the happiness of others. It can be an object sought on the basis of inclination, but it need not be sought on this ground alone. Is it, then, an object of inclination? Does it have only a conditioned value (even though it is an end everyone ought to adopt)?

At this point one may quite reasonably insist that happiness cannot be of absolute, or unconditioned, value. The reason is that it is dependent on *some* inclinations, viz., those of the person to be made happy. This is correct. Kant does hold that the happiness of others is an *intrinsic* value in the sense of having a value which is not limited merely to its worth as a means, but he does not claim it to be an *absolute* value, since it is obviously conditioned. It is of interest that while in the early part of his discussion Kant says that the end-in-itself must have absolute value, later in his account, with the development of the positive conception of objective ends, the possession of intrinsic value is deemed sufficient.

But the central contention that an object of inclination can also be an object of reason must be retained. If this is true, Kant's argument cannot show that any object sought on the basis of inclination possesses only conditioned value. What could at most be shown is that an object sought *only* on the basis of inclination has only relative value. But even this seems to be quite dubious. One may seek his own perfection and thus have the development of a good will as one of his goals even though he does so only because of inclination. Of course such a person would inevitably fail to achieve that end; in order to have a good will (according to Kant), one must do that which is right *because* it is rational and right. But it nonetheless could be one of his ends.

There is still another troublesome feature of the argument. Kant's claim that "the value of all objects that can *be produced* by our action is always conditioned" does not follow from that which comes before it. An object could be produced by someone because reason, rather than inclination, motivates him. Moreover, the value of an object that could be produced or promoted could be absolute regardless of why it is sought or whether it is sought. The most promising candidate for such an object is the good will. Kant clearly regards the good will as having unconditioned, or absolute, value. But at the same time, it is an object which can be an end of the will and thus can be promoted through willing and acting.

There is an apparent conflict in Kant's claims about absolute value. On the one hand, he appears to hold that only persons with a good will have unconditioned value. On the other hand, he says that *each* man, by virtue of his possession of a will, is an end-in-himself. The latter is clearly the more plausible interpretation of the principle of personality, for this principle applies to our treatment of all men: we are permitted to treat no man— even one who is morally unworthy—as a mere means. Each human being, by virtue of his status as a rational agent, must serve as a limiting condition for the adoption of our subjective ends. In this way each man becomes an objective end. Thus the most plausible interpretation is that both the good will and persons (as rational agents) have absolute value. But then Kant's argument is unsound because it is not true that unless *all* persons as rational agents (and thus as objective ends) have unconditioned worth, "nothing at all of *absolute* value would be found anywhere."

In ruling out objects that *can* be produced as candidates for objective ends, Kant also excludes those which *ought* to be produced or promoted. Thus the positive conception of man as an end-in-himself is eliminated from consideration. It is only afterward, with a wholly different set of arguments, that he attempts to demonstrate man's status as an end which ought to be realized or advanced.

Kant wanted to establish the dignity or unconditioned worth of all human beings. But he also desired to provide objective ends for human volition in order to supplement the form provided by the principle of universality. The tasks are combined in the development of the second formulation of the categorical imperative. A puzzling result of this effort is that human beings —entities who are "already in existence" or "self-existent"— are referred to as ends. Whereas earlier he appeared to rule out ends completely, he later settles for "objects" of this peculiar sort. Indeed he believes them to be absolutely essential for morality.

Kant's notion is puzzling because of our ordinary understanding of what ends are and because of the normal or standard use of the word 'end.' Ends are most commonly thought of as that which one seeks to bring about or achieve through action. It is in this sense that ends are contrasted with means. A cursory look at Kant's principle may leave the impression that we are being told that we ought to make persons the ends of our actions. This would be a mistaken interpretation of Kant's meaning. For the end-in-itself cannot be something which is producible. Human beings are ends, then, of a rather strange sort. They are "self-existent" ends.

Despite these difficulties, the underlying idea responsible for what Kant says is of central importance. Objective ends must have absolute value. But man himself is the only thing (Kant claims) which possesses this sort of value. From these two points he is able to conclude that man alone can be an objective end. Since this is what it means for something to be an end-in-itself, man must be the end-in-itself. Human beings thus become the content, or matter, for the moral law. I shall argue in a later chapter that this only appears to provide the object for the will.

This discussion indicates a kind of tension in Kant's overall position. It is indeed strange to say that man is an end. But if he is not the end-in-itself, then what could be? Nothing else has the supremely important and absolutely necessary qualification for being an objective end: only persons have unconditioned value. As we shall see, Kant later loosens some of his requirements and allows for objective ends which are not self-existent and which do not have absolute value.[2] Furthermore, he claims

---

2. Happiness is an objective end which does not have absolute value. Perfection does have such value, but, like happiness, it is not self-existent.

that virtuous actions themselves have an unconditioned value. The tension is thus relieved. Tension of another sort, however, is created. For Kant persists with his core notion and identifies the seeking of these positive objective ends—perfection and happiness—with the treatment of man as an end-in-himself. In so doing, he provides a different conception of objective ends, and consequently, a different conception of man as an end. For now humanity *can* be adopted and sought as an end of action. Though this is also paradoxical, humanity (or human nature) can be produced and thus be the product of the will in moral activity.

RATIONALITY AND MAN'S STATUS AS AN END

Kant's conception of man as an end-in-himself may be further illustrated and clarified by an examination of another of his arguments:

If then there is to be a supreme practical principle and—so far as the human will is concerned—a categorical imperative, it must be such that from the idea of something which is necessarily an end for every one because it is an *end in itself* it forms an *objective* principle of the will and consequently can serve as a practical law. The ground of this principle is: *Rational nature exists as an end in itself.* This is the way in which a man necessarily conceives his own existence: it is therefore so for a *subjective* principle of human actions. But it is also the way in which every other rational being conceives his existence on the same rational ground which is valid also for me; hence it is at the same time an *objective* principle, from which, as a supreme practical ground, it must be possible to derive all laws for the will. (*GW* 96)

It is important to guard against certain ways of misunderstanding these remarks. Kant is not saying that I ought to treat others as ends because I treat myself as one. Nor is the argument analogous to Mill's reputed claim that the general happiness is desirable on the ground that each man desires his own happiness.[3]

3. See John Stuart Mill, *Utilitarianism,* chap. 4. There has been much discussion concerning whether Mill actually committed some sort of fallacy in this argument.

Kant's argument is similar to, but also crucially different from, one which he offers later for the duty to seek others' happiness. The latter is as follows: since each man by nature wills his own happiness, there would be a "contradiction in his will" if he did not also will the happiness of others. This argument is based on the principle of universality. But Kant's claim that others are to be treated as ends in the negative sense does not rest on the universalization requirement. It is based, rather, on the connection between rationality and the end-in-itself. Rational nature, Kant says, is an end-in-itself. Since I conceive of myself as a rational being, I must conceive of myself as an end-in-itself. Furthermore, each man, with his possession of rationality, has a rational ground for thinking of himself as an end. Insofar as one recognizes others to be human, he must recognize them to be rational. The same rational ground, therefore, provides each person reason for thinking of others as ends.

It is on this basis that the principle of humanity is an objective one. One should not be misled by Kant's remark that the fact that each man necessarily thinks of himself as an end makes the principle subjective. This is put forward in such a way that it may seem to be a premise, but it is actually superfluous to the argument. One may even plausibly argue that, given what Kant says in other places (including the same paragraph), the assertion is false. It is important to see why this is so.

Some human beings do not regard and treat themselves as ends. Kant himself offers examples in which persons treat themselves as mere means. He believes, for instance, that cases of suicide are such situations. Again, in Kant's view, a liar treats both himself and others as mere means: one who is an habitual liar and thus makes a practice of deception could not rightly be said to possess a (subjective) principle to treat himself as an end. Thus it is false that each man of necessity regards or treats himself this way. Instead, Kant must hold that each person *ought* to regard all persons (including himself) as ends-in-themselves, and this is what he does say in a later part of his discussion. Human beings are *in themselves* ends: this status is not dependent upon their being conceived as ends by anyone at all. (Nor is it dependent upon some degree of moral attainment: no amount of effort could help one to achieve it. It is simply not the sort of quality to be acquired through moral striving.)[4]

We must also avoid another way of misunderstanding Kant's argument. Consider the following passage from a very interesting article by Pepita Haezrahi:

> . . . the same complex of circumstances and conditions which assures me of the certainty of my own freedom and moral responsibility, assures other rational beings of *their* freedom and *their* responsibility. Yet, as we must stress, no point in this argument necessarily implies an assurance for men of each other's freedom and moral capacity. In other words, the inductive assumption, or even an established fact that each rational being regards himself as possessed of dignity, on the same ground and for the same reasons that all other rational beings regard each himself as possessed of dignity, does not involve a logical necessity for rational beings to regard *each other* as possessed of dignity. This, however, is the decisive test for a general recognition by rational beings of the universal application of the dignity of man.[5]

Haezrahi rejects Kant's argument on the grounds that knowledge of freedom and rationality is possible only in one's own case and that one cannot have a basis for claiming others to be ends-in-themselves. She grants that in one's own moral experience one can become certain of his autonomous personality. But, she says, "this experience is as we have seen of necessity limited to my own person. It can therefore assure me of my own freedom, my own moral responsibility, and therefore of my own dignity and worth, but not of the dignity of others. It is, however, the *dignity of others that is in question* if I am to limit my own freedom out of a respect for theirs."[6] It should be noted that the concept of freedom is nowhere mentioned in Kant's statement of the argument. At this point he rests the claim that men are ends-in-

---

4. Kant at the same time regards morality or virtue as having a dignity or worth of its own (*GW* 103–4).

5. Pepita Haezrahi, "The Concept of Man as an End-in-Himself," in *Kant: A Collection of Critical Essays,* ed. Robert Paul Wolff (Garden City, N.Y.: Doubleday, 1967), p. 292.

6. Ibid., pp. 297–98.

themselves solely on the basis of their possession of rationality.[7] One additional consideration is essential to a proper evaluation of Haezrahi's criticism. We must assume that, with regard to the negative conception, man's dignity and his status as an end-in-himself imply one another.[8]

I shall try to show both why Haezrahi's interpretation is misguided and why Kant's argument is plausible. It is a fundamental mistake to characterize the problem of the argument in terms of a difference between one's knowledge in his own case and what he can know about others. With what Kant provides as a premise—the claim that human beings are rational agents—one may derive a conclusion applicable to everyone, and thus conclude that all men have dignity. If this were to fail, one could not draw a conclusion about dignity with respect to anyone: one's own case is not special. From Kant's statement of the argument it is clear that he believes that there is an essential connection between the possession of rationality and the possession of dignity.

At this point the objector (e.g., Haezrahi) may insist that knowledge of rationality is limited to one's own case. Since this is so, the objector may continue, one can be certain only of the fact that he himself has dignity. This mode of argument involves a distortion of the original problem. The issue ceases to be whether other men have dignity and becomes the more basic one of determining whether certain other creatures are actually men. The problem thus becomes an epistemological one and the question is the following: How can one *know*, except in his own case, that a creature is a human being, a rational animal?

Haezrahi has transformed Kant's argument, and in the process, radically misconstrued it. After this transformation the crucial question concerns the knowledge that others have minds and are rational agents. Just as skeptical positions have been

7. The concepts of freedom and autonomy (*GW* 103, 115–16) will be utilized in later chapters to support further Kant's claims about human dignity.

8. This is not true of the positive conception. Seeking the happiness of others is to treat them as ends, but happiness does not have dignity. It possesses only a relative or conditioned worth.

derived through insistence on a privileged access in one's own case, Haezrahi's purported refutation begins with the contention that one can be certain only of his own rationality and freedom. It is then only a short step to the conclusion that one has no grounds for attributing dignity to anyone other than himself. This is accomplished through claims about the unique character of the knowledge of one's own dignity. The way of acquiring this knowledge is not analogous to any supposed "knowledge" of others' dignity: one cannot have a personal experience of others' freedom and rationality. It is thus concluded that one is doomed (that is, if he wishes to be reasonable) to be skeptical about claims that others have dignity.

One way of dealing with these matters would be to conduct an investigation of the problem of other minds. There is actually no need for this, however. The merits and defects of skeptical arguments about human dignity need not seriously concern us here. Kant's intention is not to show that other creatures possess freedom and rationality. He is concerned from the outset with what he calls "rational natures"; he assumes that there are such beings and is not interested in trying to prove that they exist.

His argument may be summarized as follows: since all rational beings have a valid ground for regarding themselves as ends, each must regard all other rational beings as having dignity (or as being ends-in-themselves). The success or failure of this argument does not hinge on whether or not there are in fact any other rational beings. The point, rather, is that *if* there are such beings and *if* one recognizes them as being rational, then (in order to be reasonable) one must regard and treat them as ends-in-themselves.[9]

Kant's argument must stand or fall on the validity of his claims regarding the connection between rationality and dignity. If no link between these can be established, he cannot show that men are ends-in-themselves. He begins the argument with the assertion that "rational nature exists as an end-in-itself"

---

9. Kant's claim is as follows: (x) $(Rx \supset Dx)$, or "for all x, if x is rational, then x has dignity." It is not this: $(\exists x)$ $(Rx \cdot Dx)$, or "there is an x such that x is rational and has dignity."

(*GW* 96); this is said to be the "ground" for the principle of humanity. He evidently believes that without this he cannot show that we have a duty not to treat men as mere means. Again, man's rationality is an essential factor in establishing the end-in-itself.

But what is the basis of the connection between rationality and dignity? Kant's claims can be rendered plausible by recalling what he means by "objective ends" in the negative sense. His concern, as the context makes abundantly clear, is with the notion of man as a self-existent end. The sense in which humanity can and ought to be made the end or purpose of action is of no importance at this point: "humanity is conceived, not as an end of man (subjectively)—that is, as an object which, as a matter of fact, happens to be made an end—but as an objective end—one which, be our ends what they may, must, as a law, constitute the supreme limiting condition of all subjective ends and so must spring from pure reason" (*GW* 98). A key phrase is "supreme limiting condition." Man is an objective end in the sense of a limiting condition for all (subjective) ends. He is also considered to be a condition limiting the use of means. And it is for this reason that persons are not to be treated merely as means: "a subject of ends, namely, a rational being himself, must be made the ground for all maxims of action, never *merely* as a means, but as a supreme condition restricting the use of every means—that is, always also as an end" (*GW* 105). This idea of a limiting condition helps to provide the required link between rationality and the end-in-itself. For to be an end-in-itself is simply to be a supreme limiting condition for actions and ends.

It is quite clear that Kant regards rationality as the supreme condition restricting man's willing and his acting. To be a fully moral or virtuous being *is* to be a fully rational one. There can thus be no conflict between the requirements of rationality and those of morality. What an imperfectly rational being ought to do is what a wholly rational being (such as God) in fact (and indeed necessarily) does. To be virtuous is to act as one would always act were he to have complete rational control over his inclinations, or desires. The determination to do what is right thus would involve the determination to limit one's maxims and actions by the constraints and requirements imposed by rationality.

Rationality may be thought of as an objective end serving as a supreme limiting condition. But human beings are rational agents; they may be described as "concrete embodiments" of rationality. They are of course not wholly rational. As sensible members of the natural world, they are also subject to the yearnings of the passions. Nevertheless, they possess a rational will which legislates moral laws, and they are capable of acting rightly. In a sense, then, morality is a part of man's nature. Kant sometimes speaks—in perhaps a metaphorical way—of the "moral law within" (*CPR* 90, 166). This by no means implies that persons always act rightly and have good wills; one's active, or deciding, will (*Willkür*) often fails to measure up to the demands of the legislative will (*Wille*). But man is, despite this weakness, properly understood as rational.

The connection between rationality and the end-in-itself is thus established. The end-in-itself is defined as the supreme limiting condition for all maxims, actions, and ends. But rationality must be just such a supreme limiting condition. And man is an end-in-itself because of his possession of rationality. Kant's theory of human nature is thus absolutely essential to an understanding of the principle of humanity. We must now, beginning with the next chapter, consider the connections between man's status as an end and the duty not to treat persons merely as means.

2   SHARING ENDS

Kant's doctrine of the end-in-itself plays an important role in his application of the categorical imperative. In this chapter I shall consider his examples from the *Groundwork*. It should be noted at the outset that he did not regard this work as an essay about practical moral problems. The sustained effort to apply his moral principles takes place in a later book, *The Metaphysics of Morals*. In the course of his exposition of the various formulae, however, he does attempt to give illustrations of valid applications. These are overly brief, and as we shall see, very problematic. Kant intends that his formulae provide moral guidance and grounds for practical decision. But he does not claim to have stated the principle of humanity (or any of the formulations of the categorical imperative) in a way that will make its application easy: what it requires and what it prohibits will not be wholly clear. What he does intend is to provide situations about which almost everyone would agree, in order to show that his principles meet the test of common moral judgment about ordinary moral problems.

In examining these examples, I shall use two approaches. On the one hand, what we know already about Kant's general view of man as an end will be helpful in the criticism of his examples. On the other, I shall try to find clues as to what the principle itself means from the ways in which he applies it. In this chapter I shall concentrate on his first two examples, in which he is concerned to provide cases of treating people merely as means.

A further preliminary point is of the utmost importance. Kant's principle states that one ought to treat human beings (or humanity) "never simply as a means, but always at the same time as an end" (*GW* 96). The word 'simply' is absolutely essential. Kant is not saying that it is always wrong to treat a person as a means but that it is wrong only when he is treated simply (or merely) as such. Man is to be treated "at the same time as an end." Thus, treating someone as an end is what distinguishes treating him as a means from treating him as a *mere* means. In searching for a criterion for what it is to treat persons as mere means, we shall at the same time be seeking a criterion for treating human beings as ends.

THE EXAMPLE OF SUICIDE

Kant begins with a brief discussion in which he makes the following claims about suicide:

. . . the man who contemplates suicide will ask "Can my action be compatible with the Idea of humanity *as an end in itself?*" If he does away with himself in order to escape from a painful situation, he is making use of a person merely as a *means* to maintain a tolerable state of affairs till the end of his life. But man is not a thing—not something to be used *merely* as a means: he must always in all his actions be regarded as an end in himself. Hence I cannot dispose of man in my person by maiming, spoiling, or killing. (*GW* 96–97)

In these remarks Kant provides us with almost no new information about his principle. He does not really show that it applies to cases of suicide; he only asserts that to commit suicide is to treat oneself as a mere means. His discussion provokes some important questions. Why is killing oneself a case of treating one's own humanity as a mere means? Could one not in *some* circumstances commit suicide and at the same time treat himself as an end?

Kant appears to regard all cases of suicide as cases of treating oneself merely as a means. He has not, however, given an adequate general characterization of suicide. The man in the example kills himself in order to maintain a tolerable state of affairs until the end of his life. What Kant apparently has in mind is a situation in which the person desires to avoid certain painful future experiences. But one may commit suicide in quite different circumstances. One may find himself in an extremely painful situation with no end in sight—his condition may be intolerable already.

The end achieved in taking one's own life would not, then, be the maintenance of a tolerable state of affairs, but the elimination of an intolerable one. Could a person in such a case be treating himself as an end?

In his commentary on the *Groundwork* H. J. Paton stresses the particular end sought in and achieved by the act of suicide. The relative character of the person's ends is thought to make the action wrong:

> The man who commits suicide because the disagreeable prospects of life seem to overbalance the agreeable ones is making pleasure and the avoidance of pain his final end; and in him practical reason, which is capable of realising absolute moral worth, is being subordinated as a mere means to the relative end of avoiding discomfort. If— apart from all questions of duty to others—there can be a right to commit suicide, this can be justified only on the ground that there is no longer any possibility of living a moral life and manifesting moral worth.[1]

In these sentences Paton ranges quite far beyond Kant's own very sparse remarks. He does, however, provide an interesting suggestion as to what Kant means. Unfortunately, this account of the suicidal act suffers from the same problems encountered in the examination of what Kant himself says. One who kills himself need not do so only because a careful calculation has resulted in the conclusion that his prospects (if he stays alive) are, on balance, more "disagreeable" than "agreeable." Furthermore, one's own pleasure need not be the end of the action (much less the "final" end). As mentioned before, a person may already be in an extremely painful condition. One of his purposes could quite conceivably be the elimination of pain. But it need not be his only or final end. We may even suppose that he sincerely believes the act of killing himself to be, in his particular circumstances, what he ought to do. He thus commits suicide for the reason that he believes it to be the right thing to do, as well as because he desires to rid himself of intolerable pain. Would he be treating himself as a mere means?

---

1. H. J. Paton, *The Categorical Imperative* (London: Hutchinson, 1967), p. 172.

Let us consider a somewhat more complex description of the person and his circumstances. Suppose that morality becomes the person's determinate goal. The elimination of pain is one of his ends, but it is not a sufficient motive for the action. His performance of the action is conditional on his belief that it is morally required. Otherwise he would not kill himself. The determining motive is not to rid himself of pain but to do what is right. The fact that he believes he ought to kill himself would be sufficient—even without his suffering—to get him to do so. His supreme end, therefore, may be described as "morality," or as "obedience to the commands of the moral law."

This case is not covered by Paton's description. Yet it is surely an example of suicide, all acts of which Kant apparently holds to be violations of the categorical imperative. Paton's proposal thus leaves us without an adequate criterion of what Kant means by treating others as ends and why he regards suicide as a way of treating someone merely as a means.

In the *Metaphysics of Morals,* Kant presents a somewhat different position when he suggests that not all suicidal acts are wrong: "Arbitrary *suicide* can be called self-murder (*homocidum dolosum*) only if we can show that it is generally a wrong committed either upon one's own person or also, by the destruction of one's own person, upon others (as when a pregnant woman kills herself)" (*DV* 84). In setting out his "Casuistical Questions," Kant also appears to allow for the possibility that some acts of suicide are morally justified (*DV* 86–87). Let us suppose he *does* admit that some acts of self-killing are right. What then follows concerning the application of the principle of humanity?

There are two possibilities: (1) Kant regards all cases of suicide as treatments of persons as mere means and believes some acts of treating people this way to be right, or (2) he regards all treatments of people as mere means to be wrong and considers some acts of suicide not to be cases of treating people as mere means. It is clear that the latter is the only acceptable alternative. The various formulae of the categorical imperative provide, in Kant's view, several ways of stating the supreme principle of morality. There can be no justified exceptions whatsoever to this necessary principle. It is the ultimate principle in terms of which all other moral rules and duties are to be derived and validated. We must assume, then, that Kant regards as wrong all acts of treating people merely as means.

These points suggest a general principle of interpretation. If we can determine what would justify suicide, we can also determine why some cases involve treating someone as a means while others involve treating another as a mere means. The reason for this is that all cases of justified suicide would be instances of treating someone as an end as well as a means. A clue to solving this problem of differentiation may be found in the following paragraph:

> Man cannot renounce his personality so long as he is a subject of duty, hence so long as he lives; and that he should have the moral title to withdraw from all obligation, i.e., freely to act as if he needed no moral title for this action, is a contradiction. To destroy the subject of morality in one's own person is to root out the existence of morality itself from the world, so far as this is in one's power; and yet morality is an end in itself. Consequently, to dispose of oneself as a mere means to an arbitrary end is to abase humanity in one's own person (*homo noumenon*), which was yet entrusted to man (*homo phaenomenon*) for its preservation. (*DV* 85)

The use of the word 'mere' in the last sentence is most inappropriate, for it suggests at least two things which Kant cannot possibly have meant: (1) that it would be permissible to treat oneself as a mere means to a nonarbitrary end, and (2) that it would be permissible to treat oneself as a means to an arbitrary end provided that one did not treat oneself *merely* as such.

Some of what Kant says in the paragraph above suggests that all acts of suicide are wrong; this is because any such act involves the "rooting out" of morality in one's own person. The last sentence of the quotation, however, is indicative of a quite different view: what makes certain acts of suicide wrong is the "arbitrary" nature of the ends for whose sake they are performed. If one's purpose were not arbitrary, the action presumably could not be condemned. We may formulate, then, the following tentative criterion for treating persons as mere means: *to treat a person merely as a means is to treat him as a means to an arbitrary end.* We are now, however, beset by another group of questions. What makes an end arbitrary? How does this criterion relate to the notion of treating persons as ends-in-themselves? In order to answer these questions it is essential to consider Kant's second sample application of the principle.

THE CRITERION OF SHARING ENDS

The notion of sharing in ends plays a key role in Kant's attempts to distinguish right acts of treating persons as means from wrong ones. He introduces this concept in the following passage:

> . . . so far as necessary or strict duty to others is concerned, the man who has a mind to make a false promise to others will see at once that he is intending to make use of another man *merely as a means* to an end he does not share. For the man whom I seek to use for my own purposes by such a promise cannot possibly agree with my way of behaving to him, and so cannot himself share the end of the action. This incompatibility with the principle of duty to others leaps to the eye more obviously when we bring in examples of attempts on the freedom and property of others. For then it is manifest that a violator of the rights of man intends to use the person of others merely as a means without taking into consideration that, as rational beings, they ought always at the same time to be rated as ends—that is, only as beings who must themselves be able to share in the end of the very same action. (*GW* 97)

Here Kant offers what appears to be a promising way of understanding the principle of humanity. What Kant provides in this passage appears initially to be much different from the suggestion made near the end of the last section. In this chapter and the next an attempt will be made to reveal the similarities between them. But it is first of all essential to consider some further problems of interpretation.

The following criterion may be extracted from what Kant says: *to treat a person merely as a means is to treat him as a means to ends in which he cannot share.* This statement serves two interrelated functions. It is a standard in terms of which one can determine whether someone has violated the principle of humanity. But it also provides a way of distinguishing between, on the one hand, treating a person merely as a means, and on the other hand, treating him as a means but also as an end. In order to determine whether an action violates the principle one must have the answers to two questions. First, is someone treated as a means? If this question is correctly answered in the negative, one knows that the action is not wrong (or at least, not wrong on the basis of Kant's second formula). For if one is not treated as a means at all, it follows analytically that he is not treated as a mere means. If, however, the answer to this question is "yes," one must ask a further question: can the person treated as a means share in the ends for whose attainment he serves? If he cannot, the action is wrong. If he can, the principle of personality is not violated, and (so far) one has no reason for condemning what is done.

Kant sometimes states the principle quite differently from the formulation provided above. In one place he says that the person who promises falsely treats the other *"merely as a means* to an end he does not share" (*GW* 97). This statement clearly cannot serve as a criterion for treating someone as a mere means. It renders useless the purported contrast between treating a person merely as a means and treating someone as a means to ends which he can share. Kant's remark suggests that one could treat a person as a means to an end he does not share without treating him merely as a means. If this is so, treating a person merely as a means cannot be understood as treating him as a means to an end he does not share. And then the fact that a person shares the ends of the action cannot serve as an identifying mark of the rightness of the act.

These disappointing developments leave us with no way of determining whether a case of treating someone as a means is also a case of treating him merely this way. This gives us some reason, at least provisionally, for interpreting the problematic remark as a slip. The main task—to determine what Kant means in his discussion of the second formulation of the categorical imperative—can be greatly facilitated by ignoring this particular questionable statement and concentrating on the criterion extracted above. Kant's other remarks are quite similar to the statement of that criterion. An attempt will be made later to provide a more adequate justification for the interpretation, but at this point, to treat a person as an end will be understood as treating him in such a way that he can share the ends of the action. It will be further assumed that if one treats another in this way, he cannot be treating him merely as a means (though of course he may be treating him as a means).

There is much that is unclear about the principle as presently formulated. The above account, however, does provide an initially attractive way of understanding actions in which persons are treated merely as means. Its appeal may be illustrated by considering certain rather common examples. Suppose that an employer hires a person at a mutually agreed-upon wage. In getting him to perform certain tasks, the employer treats the employee as a means. Since, however, the worker shares (at least some of) the ends for which he is treated, the employer does not treat him merely as a means. Similarly, if two people have common aims in setting up and running a business, they do not appear to treat each other merely as means, though each may benefit from the use he is able to make of the other. Furthermore, sexual relations between consenting adults might be understood as morally acceptable since, though they use each other as means, the individuals involved share the ends of the actions.

Several points should be made about these examples and about the assumptions on which they are based. The most important is that these applications do not actually reflect what Kant means by "sharing (in) ends." As a prologue to the establishment of this claim, I shall present certain considerations intended to show that the notions of sharing ends embedded in these cases are not adequate for an account of treating persons as mere means. There are at least three different ways of sharing ends (or sharing *in* purposes). A person may share in an end or goal if (1) he *benefits* from its achievement. In this sense a child could share in the purpose which his father has in going to work each morning, despite the fact that he wants him to stay at home. Even though making money may not even be an end of which the child is aware, he benefits from his father's satisfaction of that aim. Another way of sharing ends is (2) to *hold* them as one's own purposes. The man's wife shares his end of making money. It is her end as well as his, and she might even help fulfill it by, for example, waking him up in the morning and cooking his breakfast.

Another example may serve to elaborate this conception. Suppose that both Smith and his neighbor, Brown, go to work each morning in order to make money. Do they share ends? Let us suppose that they do not share ends by benefiting from each other's purposes. Though each benefits from the achievement of his own goal, neither benefits from the other's making money. Do they share ends by holding the same purpose? This question is unanswerable without ridding the phrase "holding the same ends" of an ambiguity. In one sense they do hold the same ends: each possesses the goal describable as "making money." In another sense, however, they may not have the same ends, for the end of each is subject to a different description. Smith's end is "Smith's making money," and Brown's aim is "Brown's making money."

Understood from this latter viewpoint, Smith and Brown share ends in neither of the two senses thus far delineated: they neither benefit from nor hold the same ends. But there is another sense which may plausibly be given to the notion of sharing ends. Smith may (3) *approve of* or *assent to* Brown's end of making money. This last meaning of the term is closer to what Kant means. It cannot be utilized, however, to form a completely accurate interpretation. In order to understand why this is so—and why the other meanings are not Kant's own—it is necessary to see why these notions of sharing ends are inadequate as ways of explicating the principle of humanity in its original form, viz., "It is wrong to treat persons merely as means."[2]

2. These ordinary notions of sharing ends are implicit in several discussions of Kant's principle of personality; see the following: Arthur E. Murphy, *The Uses of Reason* (New York: Macmillan, 1943), pp. 17–18, 266-67; Warner Wick, Introduction to *The Metaphysical Principles of Virtue* [Part II of Kant's *The Metaphysics of Morals*], trans. James Ellington (Indianapolis: Bobbs-Merrill, 1964), pp. xviii–xix; Leonard Nelson, *System of Ethics*, trans. Norbert Guterman (New Haven: Yale University Press, 1956), pp. 130–35; Errol E. Harris, "Respect for Persons," in *Ethics and Society*, ed. Richard T. De George (Garden City, N.Y.: Doubleday, 1966), p. 122.

Let us begin by considering the examples already mentioned. Suppose that the worker does in fact benefit from the employer's use of him as a means. In at least one sense, then, he shares the ends for the sake of which he is used. But this may be of little or no importance to the employer. He may not care at all about whether the employee benefits from the work. His sole concern may be his own interest in getting a certain job done and in making use of his employee as a means to that end. If such were the case, he might very well be treating him merely as a means, despite the fact that the employee shares in the ends for which he is treated. Indeed, from the employer's point of view, it may only be accidental that the worker shares them. The employer might even have treated him as a means although he knew the employee could not benefit from the achievement of the purposes. If so, the fact that the worker can in this particular case benefit makes no difference to the employer. It would appear, then, that the person is not treated as an end. He is treated as a means, and he shares the ends for the sake of which he is used. But is he not also treated merely as a means?

These considerations suggest that benefiting from the purposes of the action is insufficient to make a case of treating someone as a means also a case of treating him as an end. But it may be objected that we do not really have here a case of treating someone as a means to ends in which he can share. For a person could be treated as a means *while* sharing the ends achieved by the action, even though he is not *treated as* a means *to* those purposes. It could be only incidental that he shares the ends. In order for the employer to treat the employee as being able to share in the ends, the employer must intend or desire that he share them. This takes account of certain elements of the employer's internal state, whereas the earlier discussion concentrated on the merely external aspects of the situation. This brings into focus another way of interpreting the phrase "to treat a person as a means to ends in which he can share."

Despite its advantages, this interpretation is also inadequate for providing an account of the principle of personality. Suppose that the employer does desire that the employee benefit from the ends of the actions and even takes careful steps to insure that this is so. But he does not do these things because of a regard for the well-being of the employee. The employer cares about whether or not the worker benefits only so that he can make better use of him as a means. He believes that the only way in which he can get the prospective employee to work well (if at all) is to make sure that he benefits from the purposes of the work. His concern that the worker share the ends of the action thus becomes a part of the means to getting the job done. It is limited by and restricted to his desire that the employee serve as a means. From the employer's point of view the employee is very much like a complicated machine that will not work properly unless cared for in a certain way. It appears that in this case a person is treated merely as a means despite the fact that he is treated as a means to ends in which he can share.

Similar claims may be made with regard to the example of sexual relations between consenting adults. Each may be treated by the other as a mere means despite the fact that they are treated as persons who are able to benefit from the ends of the actions. The same point applies to the notion of holding the same ends. One may be treated merely as a means to ends shared in this way. Bill's end may be Mary's pleasure as well as his own, and he may treat her as a means to both. Let us suppose that her ends are also his pleasure and hers. Even if all of this were true, Bill could still be treating Mary as a mere means. He may regard her pleasure as connected in an important way with his own—that is, that he cannot really achieve enjoyment unless she receives enjoyment as well. This may be his only reason for seeking her satisfaction: it is an intermediate end which he wants to achieve because it is an indispensable means to his own ultimate aim. In this case, then, he treats her as a mere means even though he treats her as a means to ends which she holds as her own. If this is so, sharing ends in the sense of holding the same purpose cannot be sufficient for treating a person as an end. Thus, the criterion proposed for treating persons as mere means is inadequate.

The same considerations apply to the third suggested meaning for the phrase "sharing (in) ends": a person may be treated as a means to ends of which he approves or to which he assents. This may be done in circumstances such that the agent seeks the other's approval only in order to get him to serve as a means. The agent's paramount aim is to achieve his own purposes, and the person used as a means is subordinated to them. It does not appear at all plausible that the latter's mere approval or consent is sufficient to keep the case from being one of treating a person as a mere means. In the light of these points, the criterion of sharing ends as thus far analyzed appears to be most unsatisfactory.

THE INADEQUACY OF ORDINARY NOTIONS

At this point one may object that the mode of argument employed in the last section cannot show the criterion of sharing ends to be mistaken. One might insist that the cases described thus far are not really counterexamples, that is, examples in which a person is treated as a mere means even though he shares the ends for which he is treated. In order to provide further reason for rejecting the criterion, I propose to consider other cases. Some of these are Kant's own illustrations; others are ones that would be regarded by almost everyone as clear cases of treating persons merely as means.

Two previous points should be kept clear at the outset of this discussion. First of all, the criterion to be evaluated is stated in the following way: *to treat a person merely as a means is to treat him as a means to ends in which he cannot share.* Secondly, there are three possible interpretations of "sharing ends" to be considered: benefiting from ends, holding them, and approving of them. It is argued that each is inadequate for an explication of the principle of humanity. What Kant means by "sharing (in) ends" will become clearer if these points are kept in mind.

Kant intends that the principle of personality function as a moral standard in terms of which actions and practices can be evaluated. It should perhaps not be expected that *every* wrong action will be condemnable on the ground that the principle is violated; however, there are certain actions, commonly regarded as wrong or morally reprehensible, which are clearly subject to it. One of the most likely candidates is the practice of slavery. Surely, to hold people in such subjection is one way of treating persons as mere means; it may even be regarded as a paradigmatic case of such treatment. If slavery is not an instance in which the principle of humanity is violated, it is not at all clear what would be.

The problem is to determine whether the "sharing in ends" criterion is adequate to cover this sort of case. Suppose that a slaveholder treats the slave as a means to his own purpose of harvesting his crops. Suppose further that harvesting the crops is an intermediate end whose purpose is to make (for the slaveholder) a sizable amount of money. These are quite clearly aims for whose achievement the slave may be treated as a means. They are also, however, ends in which he could share. It is not impossible to envisage circumstances in which this might be true. The master could take part of the crop and give it to the slave for food. Or he could sell it and use part of the income for the slave's clothing, health care, and other needs. Although treated as a means, the slave clearly benefits in some ways from the realization of the purposes for which he serves. In this sense he shares the ends of the actions and practices. But surely he is treated merely as a means.

The issue here is partly whether the fact that he shares these ends justifies the slaveholder's keeping the person as a slave. On the basis of the criterion under consideration, it would provide a justification. While not necessarily absolutely justified or justified on the whole, the slaveholder's actions would, nonetheless, be justified *from the standpoint of the principle of personality*. As far as *this* principle is concerned, the actions are right and the practice is morally acceptable. The action, of course, may still be wrong. To say that an action is not wrong according to this principle is not to condone it (any more than saying an action is not wrong according to the rule against lying is to condone it); other principles may also apply to it. The main point is that, judged by the interpretation of "sharing (in) ends" thus far considered, the principle of humanity does not rule out slavery.

One may object that despite the fact that slavery is wrong, we do not yet have here a clear case of treating a person as a mere means. The slaveowner apparently has some degree of concern for the welfare and interests of the slave. If so, it may be argued, he does not treat him merely as a means. And if this is true, we do not actually have a counterexample that can be brought to bear against the above-stated criterion. This objection introduces a totally new conception of treating persons as ends, viz., having regard for their welfare or well-being. This may or may not be a plausible way of understanding the notion of man as an end (in circumstances, that is, such that treating someone as an end is thought to differentiate right treatments of persons as means from wrong treatments). Regardless of the merit which this view may have in its own right, however, it is not the conception of persons as ends which we are now considering, and it is plainly not what Kant means by treating persons as ends in contexts in which they are treated as means.

A fuller description of the slaveholder's actions and attitudes may serve to make it clear that he is treating the slave merely as a means. We may suppose that the only reason the master gives the slave some of the harvested crop is to make him a good worker. Food is thus provided for him only so that he can continue to be used effectively as a means. The master's feeding the slave is simply a way of getting the maximum amount of use from his harvesting "equipment," an action analogous to his treatment of certain nonhuman things used for the same purpose. He feeds corn to his horse so that the animal can be used for the same tasks—and for the same ends—as those for which he uses the slave. He spends a portion of his income for repairs on plows and for other materials needed to keep the equipment in good working order.

The slave may, nonetheless, share in the ends for which he is used as a means. He clearly shares them in the sense that he benefits from them. And the purposes may also be shared by being held as his own ends or by being accepted by him as ends that are worthy of achievement. The most reasonable thing for the slave to object to is not the ends, but the means: he should object, that is, to being treated as a mere means. Yet according to the criterion under consideration, the fact that he shares in the ends makes it impossible for him to be treated as a mere means. These points provide good reason for rejecting the criterion. If a theory of treating others merely as means cannot account for so obvious a case, then it cannot be accepted as adequate.

A similar conclusion may be reached about other clear cases of treating people merely as means. A man who kidnaps a child in order to obtain ransom money from the parents treats another merely as a means. But the child may still share in the ends for which he is treated. The child may believe that he cannot escape unharmed unless his father pays the money. He thus may desire that his father do whatever the kidnapper says. And if his belief about this matter is correct, he may certainly benefit from the kidnapper's achievement of the end. Again, we are provided with some reason to reject the proposed criterion for treating persons as mere means. We also have grounds to reject it as an interpretation of Kant's remarks about the principle of personality. Further reason for thinking it implausible as an account of Kant's view may be obtained by a closer look at what he says in his second illustration.

Kant says that the person whom one seeks to use by making a false promise "cannot possibly agree with my way of behaving to him, and so cannot himself share the end of the action" (*GW* 97). This is offered as the reason for claiming that the promiser treats the other merely as a means. But why is it impossible for the promisee to share the end of the action? Let us suppose that Smith believes that he can make Brown happy only by falsely promising to do something for him. Although Smith may be mistaken concerning the most effective means to his end, his purpose in telling the lie is to increase Brown's happiness. Surely it cannot be sensibly denied that Brown shares, in some ways, the end of the action: the achievement of the end is beneficial to him, and he also accepts the end and holds it as his own. (Indeed, he must hold it. As was noted in the last chapter, each person by nature and of necessity, in Kant's view, seeks his own happiness.)

If we accept the interpretation of "sharing (in) ends" utilized thus far, Kant's view appears to have incompatible implications. The inconsistency is among the following propositions: (1) in any case of making a false promise to another, one treats him merely as a means; (2) in some cases of false promising, the person to whom the promise is made can share in the end of the action; and (3) to treat a person merely as a means is to treat him as a means to ends in which he cannot share. From (1) and (2) the following may be deduced: (4) one may treat a person merely as a means even though he shares the ends for which he is used. From (3) we may derive the following: (5) if a person shares the ends for which he is used, he is not treated as a mere means. But (4) and (5) quite obviously conflict. Viewed in this way, Kant's position becomes incoherent.

Another problem arises with this interpretation. Understood as the interpretation requires, Kant's account contains a non sequitur. Consider Kant's remark that the promisee "cannot possibly agree with my way of behaving to him, and so cannot himself share the end of the action." Let us suppose that the promisee does object to having been told a lie and thus finds unacceptable this particular means of having his natural desire for happiness fulfilled. As in the case of the slave, he rejects not the ends of the action but the means. From the fact, then, that one cannot agree with a particular way of behaving, it does not follow that he cannot share the end of the action. But, in the context of his second application, the burden of Kant's argument that the promisee is treated as a mere means rests on just such an inference. This way of interpreting the notion of sharing in ends thus has a further unfortunate consequence.

A still more serious problem is created by this interpretation of Kant's principle. It has been claimed that one can share the ends of the action even though he cannot agree with the agent's behavior toward him. But what if the promisee *can* agree with or consent to the behavior? Kant says that he cannot possibly agree. But in one sense of agreement, this is clearly false. Suppose that the promisee's happiness is so important to him that he does not care how it is advanced so long as it is actually increased. Brown may believe that it is only by Smith's lying to him that he can achieve this end. We may even assume, with Kant, that the false promise involves Brown's being treated as a means. He may be willing to be treated in this way because he believes that the ultimate result will be in his favor. Brown knows that some promise will not be credible but nonetheless views Smith's making it as a very easy and efficient way of achieving his own aims.

The same may be true of certain attempts on the freedom and property of others. These are worthy of mention because of Kant's view that such cases are even more obvious examples of treating people merely as means. One may be willing to have his freedom strongly curtailed (by, for instance, being tied up) in being used as a means because he believes he can thereby satisfy his interests. Similarly, one may not object to having his property stolen when he believes this to be a good way of obtaining evidence against a known thief. In a sense one does consent to or agree with the action taken against him. And he does share at least some of the ends of the actions. But is he not treated merely as a means?

These examples could be expanded and elaborated in numerous ways. I see no need for this, however. Our purpose thus far has been to adduce certain consequences of a particular way of interpreting Kant's claims. We must conclude that the notions thus far considered—despite their plausibility and initial appeal as glosses of what is ordinarily meant by "sharing ends"—are inadequate for a sound account of Kant's principle of humanity. The reasons leading to this conclusion are basically twofold: (1) the proposed criterion cannot account for (and is indeed at variance with) what almost everyone would regard as clear, obvious cases of treating people merely as means, and (2) the criterion cannot account for the examples Kant himself offers. If an interpretation is to be worked out which avoids the problems thus far delineated, we must look further in order to determine what Kant means. In the next chapter I shall argue that Kant's notion of sharing (in) ends is much different from our ordinary or usual understanding of what this means.

3

THE
RATIONAL WILL

It is essential that we provide a more plausible account of what Kant means by "sharing (in) ends" in order to determine how to understand and apply the second formula. The principle of humanity is interpreted by Kant himself as declaring it wrong to treat others as means to ends in which they cannot share. In the last chapter it became clear that our ordinary understanding of the notion of sharing (in) ends could not provide an adequate account of this principle; yet Kant's own specialized, technical meaning for this puzzling concept is not at all clear from his remarks in the *Groundwork*. Since he first introduces it in that work, however, it is helpful to recall exactly what he says in his second sample application:

... so far as necessary or strict duty to others is concerned, the man who has a mind to make a false promise to others will see at once that he is intending to make use of another man *merely as a means* to an end he does not share. For the man whom I seek to use for my own purposes by such a promise cannot possibly agree with my way of behaving to him, and so cannot himself share the end of the action. This incompatibility with the principle of duty to others leaps to the eye more obviously when we bring in examples of attempts on the freedom and property of others. For then it is manifest that a violator of the rights of man intends to use the person of others merely as a means without taking into consideration that, as rational beings, they ought always at the same time to be rated as ends—that is, only as beings who must themselves be able to share in the end of the very same action. (*GW* 97)

Attention to previously unconsidered features of this paragraph may serve to provide explanations for the difficulties encountered earlier and may also be helpful in attaining a more accurate grasp of what Kant actually means.

SOME NEW PROBLEMS

In the passage quoted above there are at least two different characterizations of the "sharing ends" standard. Kant speaks alternatively of ends one "does not share" and of ends one "cannot share." This is suggestive of a possible incoherence in his position, for presumably, ends which a person *could* (under certain conditions) share would not always be ones which he in fact *does* share. Thus, a single action—depending upon whether the "could share" or the "does share" criterion is employed—could be judged in two different ways: on the basis of one interpretation it would be right, but on the other it would be wrong.

An example may make this clear. Suppose that the president of a company, Chester, seeks to make use of one of his vice-presidents. The ends he hopes to achieve are the quelling of union sentiment and the rallying of likely supporters for the current policies of the firm. The method used in the attainment of these goals is to get the vice-president, Mortimer, to make a series of highly inflammatory speeches filled with harsh invective. He will make these speeches against union organizers to various divisions in the company. Mortimer does not realize, however, just how he is being used: he is ignorant of the president's motives and does what he is told because a refusal would weaken his position in the company.

We may suppose further that Mortimer does not share the ends for the sake of which he is treated as a means. Although he is in sympathy with Chester's basic business outlook and has the same attitudes toward union agitators, he does not believe the organizers to be strong enough to be reckoned with. He also believes that support for present company policy is overwhelming and that there is simply no need to stir up sentiment in its favor. Mortimer thus neither holds nor approves of the ends for whose realization he is being used.[1] Is he treated merely as a means?

1. This should not be taken to suggest that he *disapproves* of the ends.

According to one criterion seemingly obtainable from what Kant says, the vice-president *is* treated as a mere means, and therefore, the principle of humanity is violated. For Chester treats Mortimer as a means to ends which he does not share. The reasons he does not share them are admittedly quite peculiar; if it were not for his ignorance of the president's motives and his false beliefs about existing economic power, he most assuredly would share Chester's purposes. The fact remains, however, that he does not. A natural tendency at this point is to shift to another criterion also extractable from the Kantian text. Despite the fact that Mortimer does not share the ends, he certainly *could* do so. This might be thought sufficient to insure that (however reprehensible his actions may be from some other point of view) Chester is not treating the vice-president as a mere means.

It is not hard to envisage circumstances in which Mortimer would share the ends for which he is treated. One may simply suppose that he does believe that a huge, spontaneous outpouring of sentiment for present company policy is needed. He thinks that the speeches he is asked to make are appropriate and effective devices to achieve that result. It is clearly plausible that he could be led to hold these views; his ignorance about such matters could be eradicated. In a sense, then, he *can* share in the purposes of the president's actions.

If this were the case, Mortimer would not (according to the "can share" criterion) be treated as a mere means. For though he is treated as a means to ends which he does not actually share, these purposes are ones which he *can* share. He is treated as a means, but he is also treated as an end: he himself is "able to share in the end of the very same action." The act in question, then, could not properly be considered wrong on the basis of the principle of humanity. Here we have a single action which is wrong according to one interpretation of the "sharing ends" criterion, but right according to the other.

A similar point may be made with regard to the idea of benefiting from ends. According to this interpretation, it will be recalled, one is treated as a mere means if he does not (or cannot) benefit from the achievement of the ends for which he is used. We may suppose that in this sense as well Mortimer does not share in the ends of the action. Let us suppose that he delivers all of the speeches. It turns out that they are highly successful; the president's goals are achieved. There is a marked increase in support for the company, and the union organizers' position is seriously weakened. Chester therefore benefits from the achievement of the ends. But does the person who was used as a means benefit? The vice-president had agreed to make the speeches in order to win greater favor with his boss, but things do not work out that way. As a result of the speeches, Mortimer is soon regarded as no longer useful. Although he has served the company's purpose and his speeches have undermined support for the union, they have at the same time, because of their intemperance, diminished Mortimer's credibility among the company's employees. Even Mortimer's fellow executives, despite their acknowledgment of his temporary successes, believe that he has been extreme. The union organizers, incensed by his attack and the consequent damage to their cause, make getting rid of Mortimer one of their objectives. It soon becomes clear to the president that the best strategy for the company will be to remove Mortimer from his post. By making this move, Chester will appear (to the workers) more sympathetic to their needs and feelings.

Since in this case the vice-president does not benefit from the achievement of Chester's ends, it appears that he is treated merely as a means. The action, then, would be wrong. At this point, we might shift to the "can share" interpretation of the criterion. Mortimer *could* have benefited from the ends of the action under different circumstances. It is unnecessary to describe these. The point is that at least in one sense Mortimer can share in the ends. If so, he is not treated merely as a means, and the action is not wrong. Here again we have a situation in which conflicting moral judgments can be made, again because of two different ways of interpreting the "sharing ends" criterion.

This is a problem for which no clear solution seems immediately available. There is another which is closely related to it. In order to make plausible the claim that Mortimer could or can share the ends, it was necessary to envisage circumstances and consequences which were importantly different from the ones originally described—to shift, in other words, from an account of the actual situation to a different, hypothetical one. But an indication of what the circumstances could or might be is not sufficient to determine whether the person is, in some particular case, treated as a mere means.

There is still another difficulty. Kant appears to hold that one is treated as a mere means if and only if it is impossible for him to share in the ends for which he is used. The following portions of the paragraph on the second sample application are of relevance here: "For the man whom I seek to use for my own purposes by such a promise cannot possibly agree with my way of behaving to him, and so cannot himself share the end of the action. . . . [Rational beings] ought always at the same time to be rated as ends—that is, only as beings who must themselves be able to share in the end of the very same action." Let us suppose that Kant holds that if there is a possibility of the person's sharing the purposes, he is not treated merely as a means. What sort of possibility is involved here? The interpretations of "being able to share ends" which have thus far been considered lead easily to a discussion in terms of logical possibility. This is reflected in our attempt to envisage changes in the circumstances of the original case such that Mortimer can or could share the ends.

On the basis of this interpretation it presumably does not matter that the envisioned circumstances are highly improbable; the possibility of their occurrence is sufficient. But this surely cannot be what Kant intended, for then it would be almost impossible to get a clear application of the principle of humanity. In almost every case of treating people as means, there is no contradiction involved in envisaging a different set of circumstances in which those persons hold, approve of, and benefit from the ends of the actions. Understood in this way, Kant's principle could not adequately serve as a standard for judging particular actions right or wrong.

But if Kant did not mean "logical possibility," what did he mean? Just how are his rather puzzling claims to be understood? I shall suggest an interpretation which avoids these problems. This new account involves three basic changes from the notions underlying the previous discussion. First of all, a new conception of sharing (in) ends will be introduced. What Kant means by this is variously describable as "rational agreement," "rational willing," and "consent as a fully rational being." With this interpretation it is possible to bring Kant's second formula more fully into line with other key elements of his moral theory.

A second alteration concerns the notion of possibility. The sort of possibility relevant to the principle of humanity is what may be called "moral possibility." A person is used as a mere means only if it is morally impossible for him to hold the ends for which he is treated, and this can be determined only by ascertaining whether the aims of the action are themselves morally acceptable. Thus I shall develop a new way of understanding what a person "can share."

The third change in interpretation is closely related to the other two. I shall contend that, using the new conception of sharing ends, there is actually no basic conflict in Kant's position between what a person can share and what he does share. What a person, as an individual in possession of autonomy, *does* share is precisely the same as that which he *can* share as a being capable of rational willing but also affected by sensible desires.[2]

The plausibility and attractiveness of this proposed way of understanding Kant are partially based on the fact that the former difficulties are both explained and eliminated. In a later section of this chapter I shall provide a more complete discussion and justification. An examination of some problems in translation may serve as a prelude. The German word for 'share' is *enthalten*. This, however, can also be translated as 'contain', 'comprise', or 'include'. A reason for choosing one of these translations, rather than 'share', may be derived from a consideration of Kant's addition of the phrase *in sich*. In the paragraph on his second example, Kant sometimes says that the person ought to be able to "share the end." But he also says that one ought to be able to "share *in* the end."

The phrases "share an end" and "share in an end" are sug-

2. The interpretation to be developed is in some respects similar to that contained in Paton's commentary on the *Groundwork*. See Paton, *The Categorical Imperative*, pp. 165–71. My account also has some similarities to that advanced in an article by John E. Atwell, "Are Kant's First Two Moral Principles Equivalent?," *Journal of the History of Philosophy* 7, no. 3 (July 1969): 273–84.

gestive of different things. The concept of holding the end, discussed earlier, fits more closely with "sharing ends," while the concept of benefiting from the end fits better with "share in an end." The phrase "share in an end" is somewhat awkward and does not have any clear or definite meaning. In contrast, "contain in" or "include in" both seem perfectly acceptable. Furthermore, "contain" and "contain in" have the same connotations; the addition of the word "in" does not change the meaning. For these reasons 'contain' is preferable to 'share' as a translation of *enthalten*.

Another reason for preferring 'contain' to 'share' is that it fits much more closely the most plausible interpretation of Kant's second formula. The ends which one can, as a rational being, share are those which he does, as a person in possession of the legislative will *(Wille), contain within himself*. To treat a person as an end, it will be argued, is to treat him in accordance with ends which he would accept were he fully rational. These are the only ends which a fully rational being can "contain."[3]

AUTONOMOUS RATIONAL WILLS

What does it mean for someone to contain an end within himself? Kant's discussion of sharing ends in the *Groundwork* was not very helpful in determining what is involved in treating others as mere means. In order to provide an adequate account of the second formula, we must turn to a highly significant passage in the *Critique of Practical Reason*. It will then be possible to relate Kant's remarks about containing purposes to the negative conception of objective ends developed in the first chapter. In the chapter entitled "The Incentives of Pure Practical Reason," Kant makes the following statement:

The moral law is holy (inviolable). Man is certainly unholy enough, but humanity in his person must be holy to him. Everything in creation which he wishes and over which he has power can be used merely as a means; only man, and, with him, every rational

3. The reader may wish to consult the Royal Prussian Academy edition of Kant's works, vol. 4, pp. 429–30.

creature, is an end in itself. He is the subject of the moral law which is holy, because of the autonomy of his freedom. Because of the latter, every will, even the private will of each person directed to himself, is restricted to the condition of agreement with the autonomy of the rational being, namely, that it be subjected to no purpose which is not possible by a law which could arise from the will of the passive subject itself. This condition thus requires that the person never be used as a means except when he is at the same time an end. We may rightly attribute this condition even to the divine will with respect to the rational beings in the world as its creatures, since the condition rests on the personality of these beings, whereby alone they are ends in themselves. (*CPR* 90)[4]

The idea of autonomy emphasized in this passage suggests a different account of sharing ends. In many of the examples given in Chapter 2, there was a reliance on certain considerations of prudence or self-interest. The notion of sharing ends, in all three of the ordinary meanings offered, was linked with something's being (or thought to be) in someone's own interest. The person to whom the false promise was made, the kidnapped child, and the slave were said to be able to share (in) the ends of the actions because it was in their respective interests that these purposes be achieved. It was also assumed that one could sometimes agree to a form of behavior (what Kant calls a "way of behaving") if he found such conduct to be in his own best interests. A person's consent would then be present if he desired certain results from the achievement of the purposes.

One source of the difficulties created by this conception can be broadly stated as follows: what a person can share in is very closely linked with the particular state of his desires or inclinations. Having a certain inclination is made sufficient for sharing in a certain end. But in the passage from the second *Critique,* reason, not inclination, is introduced as the determining factor in what a person can share. *One can share in that which he can rationally will.* The objects of rational willing are those maxims, actions, and ends which a person would necessarily will were it not for the influence of the inclinations.

It is important here to consider a few points about Kant's

4. See the Academy edition, vol. 5, p. 87.

doctrine of the will which are essential to a sound understanding of the passage from the *Critique of Practical Reason*. In Kant's moral philosophy there are two basic conceptions of the will, conveniently referred to as *Wille* and *Willkür*.[5] Wille is closely associated with man's moral autonomy; Willkür is related to man's capacity for making decisions. Wille is the *legislative* will; Willkür is the *active* will. The will is thus regarded by Kant as both "practical reason" and "the faculty of desire." Wille is linked to man's rational nature as the source of the moral law. Willkür is bound up with man's status in the world as a natural being (as well as a rational one) who must decide what to do, what ends to seek, and what maxims to adopt.

We may distinguish between these concepts more sharply by referring to points already made. Kant claims that each person has a duty to seek the happiness of others (*DV* 53–54). Each man, however, is autonomous: he has an obligation to obey only those laws which he himself legislates. It is obvious that every person does not in actual practice will or seek the happiness of others. Nonetheless, Kant must hold that there is a sense in which every man *does* will a maxim to seek this happiness. His concept of Wille provides a way of specifying this sense more precisely. On the other hand, Kant believes that each man by nature wills his own happiness (*GW* 85–86, 98). The use of the word 'will' with respect to happiness is suggestive of man's Willkür. The objects of the Willkür are what one actually does will or decide on. They are related to subjective ends and principles, while the objects of the Wille are bound up with objective ends and principles.

The moral law, it will be recalled, is said to be "within." Since Kant claims that one has a duty to seek others' happiness, he must (for the sake of consistency) hold that doing so is in accord with Wille. Willkür varies as a matter of empirical fact

5. This discussion of Kant's concept of the will is based partially on the suggestions of Lewis White Beck. See Lewis White Beck, *A Commentary on Kant's Critique of Practical Reason* (Chicago: University of Chicago Press, 1960), chap. 11; and idem, "Kant's Two Conceptions of the Will in Their Political Context," in *Studies in the Philosophy of Kant* (Indianapolis: Bobbs-Merrill, 1965), pp. 215–29.

with each person. What one person wills in this sense may often differ markedly from that which others will. But the Wille cannot differ from one person to the next. Its objects are universal ethical principles, objectively acceptable ends, and morally right actions.

Attention to the word 'rational' is helpful for a further understanding of these two notions. Man's Wille is always rational: because of the rational character of its objects—moral maxims, actions, and ends—it could not be otherwise. This is derived from Kant's general conception of morality, which specifies that a moral rule or person is a rational one, and that only a rational law or human being can be moral. Since man's Wille is inextricably bound up with his autonomy as a rational being, it is possibly misleading to speak of a particular person's Wille as rational. It *must* have this quality.

The somewhat misleading character of this manner of speaking is perhaps also partially due to another use of the word 'rationality'. In the sense in which this term is associated with Wille, all men are always rational beings. In another sense, however, the use of the word 'rational' suggests a certain kind of achievement. One can strive to be rational by seeking to make all of his maxims (subjective principles) rational ones. Similarly, one can endeavor to make his decisions more rational. One's Willkür may or may not be (in any given situation or over a certain period of time) rational. The Willkür is a will which can be developed or improved: one can become more rational and thus become a better person. I suggested earlier that each individual's moral task is "to make subjective principles of volition objective ones." This may now be described in another way. The task of the person who seeks to be virtuous and to act rightly is to bring his Willkür (his deciding or active will) into line with the requirements imposed by his Wille (his legislative will).

The paragraph from the second *Critique* quoted above contains a strong emphasis on the will and on autonomy. Kant says that "every will . . . is restricted to the condition of agreement with the autonomy of the rational being, namely, that it be subjected to no purpose which is not possible by a law which could arise from the will of the passive subject itself." There is nothing particularly unusual or surprising about this remark in the light of Kant's general conception of morality. According to this view one must not violate the autonomy of rational beings. All of one's purposes are to be limited in accord with the requirements of the moral law. And all particular moral laws enjoining, prohibiting, and permitting specific actions must be legislated by all men as rational agents. In view of the connection established between Wille and man's autonomy, the Wille is the legislative source of all moral rules. Thus only such laws as man legislates in accord with his autonomy can "arise from the will of the passive subject itself."

It is significant that Kant's remarks link treating a person as an end-in-himself quite directly with acting within the limits set by the autonomy of his will. The context makes it absolutely clear that to treat a person as a mere means is to "subject" him to some purpose not in accord with the rules legislated by Wille. If one subjects another to a purpose which is morally acceptable according to the rational will, one treats him as an end-in-himself and not merely as a means. An action, then, which involves the treatment of someone as a means to a rationally legislated end can never be wrong on the basis of the principle of humanity.

But how do these points relate to Kant's remarks in the *Groundwork* about sharing, or containing, ends? We may extract from the foregoing discussion the following criterion for treating persons as mere means: *to treat someone merely as a means is to treat him as a means to an end which is at variance with the autonomy of his will.* This criterion may be understood as equivalent to the standard elicited from the *Groundwork,* viz., "to treat a person as a mere means is to treat him as a means to an end in which he cannot share." If they are equivalent, the only sort of sharing, or containment, relevant to Kant's principle is of a distinctly rational nature.

As a natural or sensible being, one can share whatever he happens to desire or find in his own self-interest. But the conception of the will associable with this sort of sharing is Willkür. If this were Kant's intent in these passages, he could rightly be interpreted as claiming that one ought not to treat a person as a means to any ends except those which are in accord with that person's particular Willkür. A single action could then be wrong if done to one person but right if done to another. Suppose that one treats two persons as means to the same end. One of these individuals may desire the realization of this purpose, while the other (because he has aims which conflict with it) rejects it. The agent would be treating the first as an end but the second as a mere means. Given what we already know about certain key elements of Kant's ethical theory, it seems clear that Kant could not embrace this consequence. It is at variance with his basic conception of morality and with the general structure of his moral principles. For it makes the rightness or wrongness of an act dependent upon the particular inclinations of sensible beings in the phenomenal world.[6]

There is another reason for rejecting this interpretation. Kant says unequivocally that the purposes for which persons are treated as means must "agree" with man's autonomy. It is fundamental in Kant's moral philosophy that many of one's actual desires may lead one to seek merely natural purposes which do not accord with rationally legislated laws arising from the wills of rational beings. An end willed by Willkür may conflict with the moral demands of Wille and thus may not be rational. Whatever ends one may share because of his Willkür are to be limited to and conditioned by the Wille. This being the case, what one shares as a result of his particular inclinations cannot be determinate with respect to whether he is treated as an end. Otherwise, he could be treated as an "end" even though he is subjected to a purpose which is *not* possible by a law arising from his will as an autonomous agent. Given what Kant says quite explicitly in the second *Critique,* this is impossible.

If we are to develop an interpretation consistent with the fundamental tenets of Kant's moral theory, we must conclude that the essential factor in applying the second formula is a

6. A possible difficulty here is posed by Kant's claim that one has a duty to seek the happiness of others. The inclinations play a significant role in the determination of whether this duty is fulfilled, since what will make a person happy is based in part on what he desires. This duty, of course, is an imperfect, indeterminate one. These matters will be discussed further in Chapter 6.

determination of what one can share *as a rational being.* We can now see more clearly why 'contain' is better than 'share' as a translation of *enthalten.* 'Share' is suggestive of what a person actually holds, accepts, or desires; 'contain' can be more plausibly related to the "moral law within." According to this interpretation, what a person "contains within himself" are those maxims and ends which are morally acceptable. In Kant's view, such maxims and ends must consist of precisely the same set of principles and purposes which are legislated by all rational beings, that is, only those principles which can be in accord with man's autonomy. These maxims and aims are the only ones which are "possible by a law which could arise from the will of the passive subject itself."

From these considerations we may derive several alternative ways of stating Kant's second formula. To treat a person as a mere means is to treat him as a means to an end in which he cannot, as a rational being, share. It is also to use him as a means to an end which is itself morally unacceptable. It is, alternatively, to treat someone as a means to ends which a rational being cannot agree to (in the sense of 'rationality' associable with Wille). And it is to treat him as a means to ends which a fully rational or moral person *would* agree to (in the sense of 'rationality' connected with *Willkür*). Still another way of stating Kant's principle is as follows: one ought not to treat others as means to purposes which they cannot will, or for the sake of ends conflicting with laws which they can will. All of these statements are, if not equivalent in meaning, at least *extensionally* equivalent. The actions required, permitted, or prohibited by one of them will be the same as those required, permitted, or prohibited by the others. Like cases will be treated in precisely the same ways with no conflicts among them.

Morally Acceptable Ends

The essential factor to be considered in determining whether an individual treats another as an end is the rational will. It is important to distinguish the rational will, as understood in this context, from the good will. Man's status as an end-in-himself is not dependent upon the possession of a will which is good, but is linked, rather, with his autonomy. And the latter is due to his possession of a rationally legislative Wille, not of a morally good Willkür.

It must be admitted that Kant does make remarks suggestive of the good will in the second *Critique* passage. He says, for example, that "man is certainly unholy enough, but humanity in his person must be holy to him" (*CPR* 90). But he obviously does not also mean that all men are completely virtuous and have a holy will. Men are not holy in the sense of having attained perfection, but rather because the moral law is contained within them, because they are autonomous. The holiness of humanity is derived from the fact that man is both author of and subject to the moral law, which itself is holy.

These two forms of rationality and holiness must not be confused. The following passage from Paton's commentary appears to exhibit such a confusion:

> An objective and absolute end could not be a product of our will; for no mere product of our will can have absolute value. An end in itself must therefore be a self-existent end, not something to be produced by us. Since it has absolute value, we know already what it must be—namely, a good will. This good or rational will Kant takes to be present in every rational agent, and so in every man, however much it may be overlaid by irrationality. Hence man, and indeed every rational agent as such, must be said to exist as an end in itself, one which should never be used simply as a means to the realisation of some end whose value is merely relative.[7]

Paton identifies the rational will with the good will. This is very misleading. A good will is, of course, always a rational one. And there can never be any conflict between what a good will does (or wills) and what rationality requires. The rational will, however, is best thought of as the Wille (or legislative will), while the good will is least confusingly regarded as a good Willkür (or active will).[8] The good Willkür is not, as Paton claims Kant

7. Paton, *The Categorical Imperative*, pp. 168–69.
8. A problem arising from this interpretation is that in his early discussion of the good will in the *Groundwork*, Kant uses the word *Wille*

holds, present in everyone. Only the Wille, which is the same for all rational agents, is contained within all human beings. A good or rational Willkür must be developed. It is by the development of such a will that one becomes more virtuous. If Kant were taken to mean that all men possess a good Willkür, one would have to interpret him as claiming that all men are virtuous. And this is something which, besides being manifestly false, Kant most certainly did not believe.

Interpreting the second formula on the basis of the rational will enables us to handle issues and difficulties encountered earlier. In the passage from the second *Critique* there is a sharp contrast between being treated merely as a means and being treated as an end. This was found not to be true of certain claims in the *Groundwork*. There we confronted such troublesome phrases as "merely a means to an end he does not share" (*GW* 97). In the *Critique of Practical Reason,* it becomes absolutely clear that one cannot at the same time be treated as an end and as a mere means. And Kant is unambiguously explicit in the contention that it is always wrong to treat people as mere means. He says, as we have seen, that the "condition of agreement with the autonomy of the rational being" requires "that the person never be used as a means except when he is at the same time an

---

and speaks of "ein guter Wille" (*GW* 61–62; Academy edition, vol. 4, p. 393). As Beck has pointed out, however, Kant is not always consistent in his use of the terms *Wille* and *Willkür*. Sometimes he uses one when he should have used the other. It is clear, I believe, that in speaking of the good will, Kant does not mean the legislative will in virtue of which rational agents possess autonomy (and which is sometimes identified with practical reason). In one sense this legislative will could not fail to be "good": as the source of morality in autonomous agents, its willing must of necessity be good or right. Furthermore, it is only a deciding or active will that could be developed or improved. And Kant does think of becoming virtuous as the development of such a will. On *Wille* and *Willkür* see also John R. Silber, "The Ethical Significance of Kant's *Religion,*" Introduction to Immanuel Kant, *Religion within the Limits of Reason Alone,* trans. Theodore M. Greene and Hoyt H. Hudson (New York: Harper & Row, 1960), pp. lxxix–cxxxiv.

end."[9] This also makes evident his view that treating persons as means is not always wrong. It is wrong only when one does not treat them as ends. To be treated as a means without being treated as an end is to be treated merely as a means.

Reconsideration of another matter may provide a further indication of the merits of the interpretation. Kant's remarks in the *Groundwork* were found to be quite confusing because of his claims about what a person "does share" and what he "can share." Different moral consequences seemed to result from these apparently divergent ways of understanding the criterion of sharing ends. The new account provides a way of resolving this conflict, for there is no basic difference between what a person can share and what he does share in the light of suggestions derived from the second *Critique* passage. To be treated as an end, a person must be treated only with regard to purposes which he can, as an autonomous rational agent, share, or contain. A person can contain within himself all maxims and purposes which are in accord with the moral law. He cannot contain, or share, any morally unacceptable ends.

I have considered the view that a person shares certain ends in having desires that they be realized. This conception of sharing must now be rejected. For ends which a person does as a natural being share may be purposes which as a rational being he cannot share. From the standpoint of rationality, however, there is a sense in which a person does not share anything which he cannot share. A person can share all those, and only those, maxims and purposes which are in accord with his rational will (Wille). But these maxims and purposes are ones which, as an autonomous rational agent, he does share. All men do in fact share, as rational beings, the same ends and principles. This sort

9. The last phrase may be misleading. Instead of "except when he is at the same time an end," Kant must be understood to mean "except when he is at the same time treated as an end." All rational beings *are* ends-in-themselves irrespective of whether they are treated as ends or as mere means. It is because of their status as ends that they are to be *treated as* self-existent ends limiting the use of means.

of containment is independent of the state of their particular desires.

Men as autonomous agents have a kind of homogeneity—their rational purposes do not vary. Furthermore, the maxims and purposes associated with the rational will are permanent: they remain the same no matter what sorts of sharing take place at the merely phenomenal level. We are thus justified in concluding that there is no basic conflict in Kant's remarks about what one "does share" and "can share." Both kinds of sharing are properly understood as being of a rational nature. The relevant ends are what one can share as a rational being. But what one can share in this sense is what one does contain within himself as an autonomous agent in possession of Wille. The interpretation thus gains plausibility by rendering consistent important aspects of Kant's doctrine of the end-in-itself.

In Chapter 2 several examples were introduced in order to show that a person could be treated merely as a means even though he shared the purposes for whose realization he was used. In some of these cases it was suggested that one might quite reasonably accept the ends of an action but reject the means. The slave, for instance, might find acceptable the end of harvesting the crop but object to being treated as a (mere) means to that goal. He would, in a sense, "will" the end of the action, but not the means. This is in apparent conflict with the following claim from the *Groundwork:*

How an imperative of skill is possible requires no special discussion. Who wills the end, wills (so far as reason has decisive influence on his actions) also the means which are indispensably necessary and in his power. So far as willing is concerned, this proposition is analytic: for in my willing of an object as an effect there is already conceived the causality of myself as an acting cause—that is, the use of means; and from the concept of willing an end the imperative merely extracts the concept of actions necessary to this end. (*GW* 84–85)

Is the slave irrational in rejecting the means? What Kant appears to have in mind in this passage are means which are necessary, or indispensable, for the attainment of the purposes of the action. Thus understood, his view might lead to the conclusion that since the use of the slave is not indispensably necessary to the end of harvesting the crop, he is not irrational in rejecting the master's means.

But the issue can be dealt with in a way which avoids the problem of what makes a particular means indispensable. The means to be considered are broadly describable as "treatments of people as mere means." The kind of situation to be envisaged is one in which a person rejects a particular means on the ground that it involves the treatment of someone merely as a means. The new interpretation provides a way of handling such cases. For if the action does involve the treatment of someone as a mere means, one cannot will its end. We may assume that, as Kant would insist, one cannot rationally will to be treated as a mere means. One can will to be treated as a means if and only if such a treatment is morally acceptable.

But what makes any treatment of someone as a means morally acceptable? The only available way of justifying such action is in terms of the end for the attainment of which the individual is treated. If this end is morally acceptable, then it is compatible with a law which could arise from Wille and one is treated as an end-in-oneself. If one is treated as an end, he is not treated merely as a means and can will that he be treated as a means. He thus can will the means to the end of the action. We can conclude, then, that if one (as a rational being in possession of autonomy) wills the end of the action, he also wills the means.

SUPREME LIMITING CONDITIONS

I argued in Chapter 1 that there are two different conceptions of objective ends in Kant's ethics. Men are objective ends, in the negative sense, because they are to serve as the supreme limiting conditions for all subjective ends (for all ends which can be made the goals of actions). They are also objective ends in the positive sense—ends which all human beings ought to adopt and to seek. I claimed that the first conception is relevant to Kant's principle of humanity in its application to cases of treating persons as means. To treat a person as an end is to make him serve as a limiting condition for one's purposes. If one does this, he cannot be treating the other merely as a means, and his action is not wrong according to Kant's second formula. However reprehensible the act may be according to other moral principles, it cannot be condemned on the basis of this principle. We may formulate, therefore, the following criterion for treating a person merely as a means: *to treat a person merely as a means is to treat him as a means while failing to make him serve as a limiting condition for one's actions and purposes.*

Any plausible interpretation of Kant's second formula must cohere with and account for this criterion. The conception of objective ends underlying it is absolutely crucial to a correct understanding of Kant's doctrine of the end-in-itself. An explanation of these features of Kant's position is provided in the following portion of the second *Critique* passage:

> [Man] is the subject of the moral law which is holy, because of the autonomy of his freedom. Because of the latter, every will, even the private will of each person directed to himself, is restricted to the condition of agreement with the autonomy of the rational being, namely, that it be subjected to no purpose which is not possible by a law which could arise from the will of the passive subject itself. This condition thus requires that the person never be used as a means except when he is at the same time an end. (*CPR* 90)

I have claimed that to treat a person in the way Kant requires is to treat him as a means only to ends which he can rationally will—to purposes to which he can, as a rational being, consent. In this way, a moral agent meets the condition of agreement with man's autonomy. The ends which a person can rationally will are the same as those which accord with laws arising from his autonomous nature. And it is precisely this sort of treatment which can be rightly described as making humanity the supreme limiting condition for subjective ends.

This point can be clarified by a thought experiment. Let us, in this hypothetical exercise, set aside all that we know about Kant's second formula of the categorical imperative. We might even assume that Kant never introduced the doctrine of the end-in-itself and that he did not claim that men ought never to be treated as mere means. In the experiment, however, we retain a basic knowledge of Kant's general moral theory. We then suppose that one is confronted with the following question: what, for Kant, is the supreme limiting condition which must restrict the adoption of all purposes which a person might try to achieve?

The most reasonable responses are very simple ones—morality and rationality. All ends which one seeks must be moral ones, and the agent who desires to do what is right will try to determine what purposes are rational. Only such ends as these can be in agreement with the moral law. According to Kant's doctrine of autonomy, however, all *moral* maxims (and only those which are moral) are self-legislated by each person as a rational agent. Only such maxims, therefore, meet the "condition of agreement with the autonomy of the rational being." If an end meets this condition, it can be rationally willed, and only if it measures up to this standard can it arise from Wille and be sought by a fully rational or good Willkür.

In the light of Kant's doctrine of autonomy, to treat either morality or rationality as the supreme limiting condition is also to treat man in this way. And this is what Kant means by treating men as ends-in-themselves (in contexts in which they are treated as means). If morality and rationality are conditions by which one successfully restricts his adoption of (subjective) ends, then the only purposes which he seeks will be rational ones. If a purpose is rational, it can be rationally willed and contained within all rational agents. But this is only another way of saying that one treats man as an end: the only purposes for which he is used are ones in which he can rationally share.

The following two criteria, then, are equivalent and are alternative, equally plausible ways of stating Kant's principle of personality: (1) to treat a person as an end is to treat him as the supreme limiting condition for all (subjective) ends, and (2) to treat a person as an end is to treat him in such a way that all purposes for which he may be used are ones which he can rationally share. The demonstration of this equivalence makes evident still another attractive feature of the proposed interpretation. It explains and illustrates the close connection between Kant's principle of humanity and his conception of objective ends, both of which are integral elements of the doctrine of the end-in-itself.

The discussion of this connection suggests another important relationship between what otherwise appear to be disparate aspects of Kant's position. A fundamental concept which seems to underlie the second formula is the notion of respect. From an initial reading of the principle, almost everyone would agree that, whatever else Kant may mean by "humanity as an end," he is saying that human beings ought to be respected. When someone is treated merely as a means, he is not given the respect to which, as a person with ends and rights, he is entitled. But Kant also says that one ought to have respect for the moral law (*GW* 68–69; *CPR* 88). What can be concluded about this variance in his claims concerning respect?

Our exploration of the concepts of a limiting condition and of rational containment suggests that in respecting human beings, one is also fulfilling at least part of what is required for respect for the moral law. Kant speaks of duty as having an origin:

> Duty! Thou sublime and mighty name that dost embrace nothing charming or insinuating but requirest submission and yet seekest not to move the will by threatening aught that would arouse natural aversion or terror, but only holdest forth a law which of itself finds entrance into the mind and yet gains reluctant reverence . . . what origin is there worthy of thee, and where is to be found the root of thy noble descent . . . ? (*CPR* 89)

In these fervent statements, Kant seems to be saying that since duty awakens reverence, its origin (which must be "worthy" of it) must also be worthy of our respect. Kant's answer to his own question should not be surprising:

> It cannot be less than something which elevates man above himself as a part of the world of sense, something which connects him with an order of things which only the understanding can think and which has under it the entire world of sense, including the empirically determinable existence of man in time, and the whole system of all ends which is alone suitable to such unconditional practical laws as the moral. It is nothing else than personality, i.e., the freedom and independence from the mechanism of nature regarded as a capacity of a being which is subject to special laws (pure practical

laws given by its own reason), so that the person as belonging to the world of sense is subject to his own personality so far as he belongs to the intelligible world. For then it is not to be wondered at that man, as belonging to two worlds, must regard his own being in relation to his second and higher vocation with reverence and the laws of this vocation with the deepest respect. (*CPR* 89–90)

It is clear from these passages that Kant believes there is an important connection between respect for the moral law and respect for human beings. He tries to make the connection explicit by focusing attention on human personality as the source of the moral law, and therefore, of duty. If it is accepted that one has an obligation to respect morality, an argument can be made that one ought to respect human beings. It is, briefly, as follows: if one does not respect human beings, he does not respect morality, for humanity is the source of the moral law. The assumption on which this argument rests is that one cannot actually respect something unless he respects its origin, or source. As a general proposition, however, this is quite dubious. Counterexamples abound. For instance, one can respect a person without respecting his parents, even though they are his "origin." Fortunately, Kant's position on respect need not be based solely on these passages in which he emphasizes the origin of the moral law.

The proposed interpretation of the doctrine of the end-in-itself can make Kant's view more plausible. We may assume provisionally that Kant regards the obligation to treat persons as ends as also involving an obligation to respect them. This is especially clear from the context in which he discusses humanity as an end in the second *Critique*. I have argued that to treat a man as an end-in-himself is to treat him in such a way that he can rationally will all of the ends for which he may be used. This is tantamount to treating him as the supreme limiting condition for one's maxims, actions, and ends.

It is in this way that one respects human beings. This kind of respect is somewhat similar to that which one might have for one's parents, a judge, or an employer. One respects these people by being willing to limit or restrict one's actions in accordance with their wishes, orders, or goals. In this sense, respect involves an element of deference. Similarly, one can respect the rights of another by limiting one's actions with regard to him, viz., by refraining from the performance of any action that would transgress those rights. In respecting human beings one limits himself by what they can rationally contain within themselves.

To complete the argument it is necessary only to raise a question whose answer is already implied in the foregoing discussion. What can a person rationally share? One can contain, as a rational being, only morally acceptable maxims and ends. In respecting a person one respects what he can rationally share, and the object of one's respect must be the moral law. We can therefore conclude that a connection between these forms of respect can be established. The interpretation accords in still another way with Kant's basic claims and shows how they are coherent.

In Chapter 2 I stated a tentative criterion for treating persons as mere means, derived from Kant's remarks on suicide in the *Metaphysics of Morals* (*DV* 85): to treat someone merely as a means is to treat him as a means to an arbitrary end. We can now see more clearly what is involved in this criterion. It is essential to consider just what ends are "arbitrary." Kant's use of this term is not our ordinary one. We usually understand an arbitrary decision or goal to be unreasoned and capricious; this suggests that it may be due to the whims of particular individuals, and therefore, subjective. But this is not what Kant means. Moreover, in our ordinary sense of the term, a decision could be arbitrary but morally acceptable or desirable on other grounds. The consequences of an arbitrary decision need not be bad. An arbitrary action could, in an objective way, be in accord with what Kant calls the moral law; it could be covered by a maxim capable of being willed to be a universal law. In Kant's usage, however, an arbitrary end is one that is not morally acceptable.

In his article "An Alleged Right to Lie: A Problem in Kantian Ethics," H. J. Paton makes this point very well. In his discussion of possible exceptions to moral rules, he distinguishes between arbitrary and justifiable exceptions. If one seeks to make an exception of his own case and if the action is not right, the exception will be an arbitrary one.[10] This is true regardless of how

10. H. J. Paton, "An Alleged Right to Lie: A Problem in Kantian Ethics," *Kant -Studien* 45 (1953–54): 190–203.

carefully the agent tries to insure that his action is rational and right—regardless, that is, of how nonarbitrary the action may be on an ordinary understanding of the word.

Paton's point suggests a connection between the arbitrary end criterion and the sharing ends criterion. Any end which is arbitrary will be a morally unacceptable one. If an end is morally wrong, it cannot be rationally contained in the will (Wille) of autonomous agents. To treat a person as a means to an arbitrary end, then, is to treat him as a means to an end in which he cannot rationally share.

4 MOTIVES, ATTITUDES, AND OBJECTIVE ENDS

The principle of personality usually elicits enthusiastic moral approval and often provides a sense of emotional uplift. This of course is not surprising. Who could deny that something called the "dignity of man" ought to be upheld? This concept does, after all, seem to underlie Kant's introduction of and emphasis upon the second formula of the categorical imperative. In his discussion of this principle, Kant also makes claims about the absolute and intrinsic value of all human beings.

One who denies the validity of the second formula may initially be thought also to reject the contention that men have dignity and value. The principle of personality thus has great weight and receives much support in ordinary moral judgment. To this extent it measures up to one test of a sound moral principle. Its initial appeal and attractiveness, however, can be diminished through a concentration on what Kant really means by certain key notions. The basic materials for this evaluation have been provided in the previous chapters. What now remains to be done is to indicate, through the utilization of what I have called the rationality interpretation, some serious defects in Kant's conception of humanity as an end-in-itself.

The difficulties on which I plan to focus may be grouped into two general areas. The first set of objections concerns certain issues involved in relating Kant's principle to cases which we would ordinarily regard as treatments of persons as mere means. Many such cases cannot, I shall contend, be explained or accommodated by Kant's second formulation of the categorical imperative. At the same time, however, I shall suggest a way in which some of these difficulties may be overcome. These points will be somewhat tentative and are based more on textual suggestions than on Kant's explicit claims. The main problem concerns what I shall call internal phenomena—the agent's motives, attitudes, and thoughts. The issues arising from a consideration of these matters are discussed in the present chapter.

The second general problem area relates to Kant's explicitly stated reason for introducing the principle of humanity. His purpose, it will be recalled, was to provide the matter, or content, for the moral law. Believing the first formulation (the principle of universality) to be crucial but inadequate by itself, he seeks an object for human volition. As we have seen, he claims that man himself (and nothing else) is a fit subject for the concept of the end-in-itself. I shall argue that Kant cannot, with the negative conception of man as an end, provide the content for morality. The next chapter is devoted to a consideration of this issue and related problems.

Unlike those in the first problem area, the difficulties in the second cannot be handled through textual suggestions. I shall try to show in Chapter 6 that Kant's positive conception of man as an end can at least partially provide the content, or object, for the will. With the introduction of perfection and happiness, Kant does offer basic ends which all men ought to have. The positive conception, however, is not very helpful for the determination of whether someone is treated merely as a means. It is for this reason that the discussion thus far has been restricted to the negative or limiting condition notion of the end-in-itself. The interpretation delineated in Chapter 3 is confined to this conception, and the material in the present chapter applies to it as well.

THE ROLE OF THE AGENT'S MOTIVES

In Chapter 2 several reasons were given for the rejection of certain ways of interpreting Kant's second formula. These reasons consisted in considerations regarding certain proposed meanings for the phrase "sharing (in) an end." I argued that a person could be treated merely as a means even though he shared the ends of the action by holding, approving of, or benefiting from those purposes. It is important to recall a few elements of the general kind of example utilized. Suppose, for instance, that Schyster marries Matilda not because he loves her but only so that he can advance his business career. He wants to take advantage of his relationship with her because she is the daughter of his employer. As things turn out, Schyster is successful. He receives promotions very rapidly and makes quite a lot of money. His abilities are so meager, however, that he would not have been successful had he not been the boss's son-in-law. He knew this from the outset, and his decision to marry Matilda was due to just such a shrewd calculation.

Such a situation appears quite clearly to be an act of treating someone merely as a means. But Matilda also shares in the ends of Schyster's actions: she receives many of the fruits of his career advancement; she also is spared the social stigma of spinsterhood. Not being at all attractive, she probably would not have otherwise received a marriage proposal. We may even suppose that, as a result of Schyster's cunning scheme, she acquires much more money than she otherwise would have gotten. Her father had always been exceedingly thrifty and strict and would never have lavished upon her the kind of wealth with which she is blessed as a result of her marriage.

In all of these ways Matilda is better off than she would have been had Schyster not developed and implemented his plan for personal aggrandizement. But despite this good fortune and the happy ending, she is treated merely as a means. Thus the benefit conception cannot account for this case. What appears to be crucially important in this example is Schyster's motivation in the use of Matilda and his attitudes toward her. He is not concerned at all with her interests or welfare except insofar as they may be keys to his own success and wealth. He *regards* her only as a means to these ends, and this appears to be relevant to a claim that he *treats* her merely as a means.

Similar points may be made with another example. Suppose that a very sick man, Hector, has what is thought to be a hopelessly incurable disease. He believes that his remaining days are quite few. A certain medical scientist, Quackenbush, wishes to perform an experiment in the hope of finding and perfecting a possible cure. In pursuit of this end he solicits Hector's cooperation and consent for the performance of very complex and extra-ordinarily dangerous surgery. The dying individual, wishing to live as long as possible but also experiencing terrible pain and realizing he does not have much time left anyway, somewhat reluctantly agrees to the operation. As things turn out, the operation is an unexpected, complete success. Hector gets well and has every prospect of many years of health. The results of the surgery are successfully applied to many other persons similarly afflicted with the disease. There is no doubt that mankind generally, as well as the person used as a means, benefits from the scientist's efforts. Quackenbush is lauded throughout the world for his "humanitarian" achievement.

But we must consider the scientist's motivation in doing the operation. We may suppose that he is driven by self-interest of the crassest variety. He does indeed wish to play a role in a major medical breakthrough, but the possible wealth and fame associated with such a discovery are his overriding aims. The surgeon even believes that the operation will be a failure with regard to curing Hector. He performs the surgery only because he believes he might gain information to be utilized in further research. When it is successful, he is actually more surprised than anyone else, for he had deceived Hector and his relatives by telling them that there was some hope of his getting well. As he sizes up the situation, his lies about this matter are necessary in order to induce Hector to submit to the operation.

Quackenbush, then, does not care at all whether Hector gets rid of the disease, except insofar as this might be related to his own self-interest. As far as he is concerned, the patient is only a means to be utilized in an experiment. He regards him in very much the same way that he thinks of the monkeys and rabbits normally used in laboratory work. Everyone probably would agree that, under the circumstances described, Quackenbush treats Hector merely as a means, despite the fact that the sick man shares in the ends of the action. Hector perhaps would not have approved of the scientist's performing the operation had he known of his wholly self-interested motivation. But he does benefit from the achievement of Quackenbush's ends and therefore, in this way, shares them.

The consideration of examples somewhat analogous to these led to a search for a different and more plausible way of understanding Kant's notion of sharing ends. The advantages of this interpretation have been delineated in Chapter 3. But while the proposed interpretation resolves some of the difficulties encountered in the other conceptions of sharing ends, there is one especially important problem not yet eliminated. We may begin by asking the following question with reference to the cases of Schyster and of Quackenbush: What, in Kant's view, is relevant and important for determining whether Matilda and Hector are treated merely as means? In accordance with the material developed in the last chapter, the essential factor is whether they can rationally contain in themselves the purposes of the actions in which they are treated as means. Only if these ends accord with laws arising from their own wills (Willen) are they treated as ends-in-themselves. If the aims conflict with any such laws, they are treated as mere means.

The ends must be morally worthwhile or acceptable. It may very well be the case that a fuller description of Schyster's and Quackenbush's purposes would reveal that they are not morally acceptable. If this were true, Matilda and Hector would be treated as means to ends which they could not rationally will and would therefore be treated merely as means. To determine precisely what ends are morally acceptable, however, would involve a lengthy investigation not contemplated here. But this is not essential to my present purpose.

The main point to be made here rests on the following presumably plausible contention: it is, in Kant's view, possible for someone to be seeking morally worthwhile ends for ethically inferior reasons. Very early in the first chapter of the *Groundwork,* Kant makes a crucial distinction between moral rightness and moral worth. The rightness of an action is dependent upon what may be called the objective features of particular situations. An act's moral worth, however, is due to certain factors which are internal with regard to the agent's state of mind (or with regard to the state of his will). A morally right action is one which is performed *in accordance with* duty, while a morally worthy one is done *from the motive of* duty (*GW* 64–66).

How does one know what his duty is? All of man's duties are somehow derivable from, and knowable on the basis of, the categorical imperative. So a right action is one which is in accordance with the categorical imperative. From this supreme moral principle one can learn what is required, prohibited, or permitted with regard to the performance of right action. An act is right if it is required by this imperative or if it is not in conflict with that which is commanded. But this is not sufficient for moral worth. In order to have this quality, the action must be done not solely from inclination but because of a motivation to do what is right. Kant clearly believes that one can act in accordance with the categorical imperative even though he is motivated, not by a reasoned determination to act rightly, but only by his natural desires (*GW* 64–69). The completely self-interested person may perhaps only by accident perform right actions: his own selfish desires may lead him to do things which are wholly in accord with the objective or external demands of the moral law.

If actions can be understood as right or wrong apart from certain kinds of motivations for doing them, it would appear to be unobjectionable to understand aims or purposes in a similar fashion. One could seek to achieve a morally acceptable (or even morally required) end even though he does so for reprehensible reasons. Kant accepts the view that human action is basically purposive. In order to determine whether a maxim can be universalized, one must consider, among other things, the purposes which it involves. And it is in terms of maxims that can be willed to be universal laws that one decides whether one's contemplated actions would be right (*GW* 88–92). If the maxim could be morally acceptable apart from the reasons one has for acting in accordance with it, then the end specified in the maxim can be morally acceptable even though one has bad motives in seeking to achieve it.

These points may now be applied to the kind of situation exemplified by the cases of Hector and Quackenbush and of Matilda and Schyster. We may simply suppose that all of the ends which the agent seeks are morally acceptable. They are thus capable of being willed (and therefore shared) by all rational beings in possession of autonomy. The agent finds, however, that he cannot achieve these goals by himself. He requires the use of another person and treats him as a means to those ends. In such a case the individual would not be treated merely as a means; he is also treated as an end. According to the interpretation thus far developed, therefore, the action would not be wrong. This is true irrespective of whether the person treated as a means actually approves of the end of the action. His present desires are irrelevant. No matter how much such a person might object to being used as a means, he would still be treated as an end. All that counts in this regard is his rational will; if the ends to be sought are morally acceptable, he can rationally share or contain them within himself.

We are now in a position to state a serious objection to Kant's view. Let us suppose, as before, that A's ends pass all of the moral tests which are available in Kant's theory. They are thus morally acceptable and rationally willed. If A treats B as a means to *those* ends, there is presumably no way whatsoever for A to use B merely as a means. But what if his attitudes toward B are very similar to Quackenbush's feelings about Hector and to the master's attitudes regarding the slave? A does not, let us suppose, care in the least about B's welfare and makes no effort to insure that B can rationally share the end of the action. He does not care, that is, whether his purpose can accord with a law which could arise from B's will (Wille). We may suppose that A considers B only as a means to his own ends. His whole concern with the other person is due to and limited by his desires to get him to function as a means.

Almost everyone would insist, I think, that A treats B merely as a means. In Kant's view as thus far presented, however, he would be treating him as an end and therefore could not be treating him as a mere means. Kant's position thus appears to suffer from some of the same difficulties which plagued the "ordinary" interpretations of the concept of sharing ends. On the basis of both analyses of the principle of humanity, certain points relating to the agent's motives, attitudes, and feelings have been left out of consideration. Kant's somewhat strict dichotomy between moral rightness and moral worth may be a plausible explanation for this consequence. The reasons and motives possessed by the agent are apparently relegated to an area in which only judgments of moral worth have a place. They appear to be neglected as unimportant to a consideration of whether an action is right, whether it is in accordance with the categorical imperative. Yet in the kind of case outlined above, an examination of these internal matters is essential to a proper description of the act of treating someone merely as a means.

THE OMISSION OF INTERNAL FACTORS

A problem with Kant's view is the difficulty in relating the principle of personality to the concept of respect. It was suggested in Chapter 3 that Kant appears to make a close connection between respect for humanity and the treatment of man as an end. I have attempted to demonstrate a certain *prima facie* plausibility for his claims by relating each of these to the moral law. To recapitulate, acting in accord with man's autonomy (as a being in possession of Wille) is to act in accordance with the dictates of the moral law. For it is as persons who are both sources of and subject to the demand of morality that men are deserving of respect.

Though this appears to be highly plausible as far as it goes, an essential aspect of the notion of respect has not yet received attention. This concept cannot be adequately analyzed in terms of the merely external aspects of an action. To respect a judge or a parent is not merely to behave in specific deferential (and thus "respectful") ways. It is also to have certain attitudes toward them or to regard them in certain ways. "To respect a person" is often properly used to mean "to think well of him."

I do not wish to claim that Kant's accounts of the concept of respect and of the principle of personality must conform to these ordinary notions. If, however, Kant's doctrine completely ignores all considerations of these internal phenomena, it cannot be very helpful either in the understanding or in the improvement of our moral beliefs about persons as ends and about the morality of treating them as mere means. For we do commonly appeal to (variations of) the principle of humanity in situations in which we believe there to be a lack of respect for persons. To treat a person merely as a means is quite naturally regarded as a way of failing to give someone the respect he is thought to deserve.

To treat persons as mere means is often to treat them in ways strikingly similar to the ways one might otherwise treat nonhuman animals or inanimate objects. (It is useful here to recall the slave example and the Hector example.) Thus, to treat someone in this way is often to ignore certain differences between human beings and other phenomena, to fail to appreciate sufficiently the unique qualities of persons. If Kant's account has no bearing on any of these matters, one may reasonably question its value either as an aid to theoretical understanding or as a guide for practical activity.

Let us return briefly to the kind of case already described. A does not care whether B shares (as a rational being) the purposes of the action. As far as A is concerned, B is only a means to his own ends. This seems to be a case in which the agent does not respect the person used as a means. If so, Kant's view cannot provide the desired connection between treating persons as ends and respecting them. For as long as the purposes of the action are objectively in accord with the autonomy of the will, one treats another as an end-in-himself.

In order to construct an even clearer case of lack of respect, it is useful to offer a somewhat fuller description of the situation. It was suggested earlier that one could do what is right by accident. We may suppose that something very much like this occurs in the treatment of someone as a means. In this case the ends pursued just happen to be morally acceptable ones. Suppose that A is a wholly self-centered individual who strives to make all his actions conform to his own self-interest. He views other people solely from this perspective; they have a significant place only in his egoistic calculations. In a particular situation A treats B as a means to one of his goals, but as things turn out, the particular purpose for which B is used can be rationally shared. (We may conveniently refer to this example as the case of the lucky egoist.)

But is it not true that A treats B merely as a means? Are we to conclude that he treats him as an end? He would have treated B as a means to his self-interested purposes even if they had not been rational and moral. And he would have done so regardless of the effects on B's welfare or interests. He clearly does not regard him as having absolute value, for the only value A considers B to have is his usefulness as a means. It is this sort of case for which Kant's doctrine, as thus far developed, cannot adequately account. I do not wish to challenge the general applicability of Kant's distinction between moral rightness and moral worth. The weakness in that distinction, however, is in its apparent exclusion of attitudes and motives—its treatment of them as irrelevant—for the purpose of determining the rightness or wrongness of the kinds of actions which have been mentioned. Perhaps not all adequate moral judgment requires attention to the attitudes and motives of the agent. Furthermore, the internal phenomena relevant to judgments of moral rightness may differ from those important to considerations of moral worth. It may be true, for instance, that although having respect for a person is sufficient to keep a treatment of him as a means from being wrong, it is not sufficient for the action's (or the agent's) possession of moral worth.

I suggested earlier that one could act in accordance with the principle of universality even though he makes no special effort (or indeed any effort whatsoever) to make his conduct conform to its requirements. One's action would then be right but not morally worthy. Kant presents his various formulae in a way which suggests that each of them may be understood in just this manner. The account suggests that one could act in accordance with the principle of humanity even though he makes no effort to do so. But while there is no difficulty, on the one hand, in saying that one acts in accordance with a maxim that can be willed to be a universal law even though he does not attempt to do so, it is quite strange indeed to say that one *treats* a person as an end-in-himself, or as having absolute value, even though he does not try to do so.

One may plausibly be said to act in accordance with the first formulation (the principle of universality) only by accident. But it does not seem reasonable to say that one can accidentally treat a person as an end-in-himself when one's selfish purposes happen to coincide with the ends of morality. These points bear a significant relation to claims about the alleged equivalency of the first two formulations of the categorical imperative. A factor lending support to the view that they are equivalent is Kant's apparent lack of concern (with respect to moral rightness) with the kinds of internal phenomena I have emphasized. I shall shortly suggest that Kant may very well have held that such phenomena are important. To the extent that this suggestion can be supported, a claim of equivalence for Formulations I and II is proportionately weakened.

In order to prepare the way for a more comprehensive examination of Kant's view vis-à-vis the relationship of the second formula to internal phenomena, we may sketch a case involving the reversal of the lucky egoist's situation. In this case C is very concerned that D rationally share all of the ends of his action and tries very hard to make sure that this is so. C does not wish D to serve as a means to his purposes unless he is certain that these goals are morally acceptable ones. We may suppose further that he knows the requirements of morality according to Kant's theory and that he tries to live up to them. He endeavors to make rationality the supreme limiting condition of his conduct. The agent also realizes that the doctrine of autonomy requires that man's Wille be in agreement with all actions and purposes. In this regard he tries to make man's rationality (and thus humanity) the limiting condition of his actions.

In trying to refrain from treating D as a mere means, he thus seeks to limit his conduct so that the pursuit of his own ends can be in agreement with D's will. With regard to the internal elements in the concept of respect, C *does* respect D as a rational being. But things do not, let us suppose, work out in quite the way he thought they would. Being morally fallible and not fully rational, he makes an ethical miscalculation. He considers the principle of universality and tries to determine whether his maxim (which itself "includes" the purposes of the proposed action) can be willed to be a universal law. After careful deliberation he decides that it can. He concludes that his purpose is morally acceptable and that D can, therefore, rationally share it as an autonomous agent. His moral struggle having terminated, he proceeds to treat D as a means to the ends in question. C, however, is mistaken. The ends he seeks are not morally acceptable, and his action, according to the first formulation of the categorical imperative, is wrong.

Does this person treat another merely as a means? According to the interpretation developed in the last chapter, he does not treat him as an end. For, like the principle of universality, the second formula appears to be restricted in its application to the merely external or objective features of moral situations. If the end of the action is not a morally acceptable one, it cannot be rationally shared by the person being used as a means. But this is a necessary feature of treating persons as ends. This being the case, C treats D merely as a means. His action must therefore be judged to be wrong on the ground that it violates the principle of humanity. (We may call this example the case of the unfortunate do-gooder.)

The difficulties created by this case may now be compared with those in the example of the lucky egoist. In the egoist's case, Kant's principle appears to be too permissive; in the do-gooder's case, too harsh. We would most likely be inclined to make moral judgments opposite to those required by a proper application of Kant's principle: that is, the lucky egoist treats someone as a mere means but the unfortunate do-gooder does not. In the former case, what Kant regards as *sufficient* for treating a person as an end does not seem to be enough. And in the latter example, what he regards as *necessary* for treating someone this way does not seem to be required.

I have noted that the lucky egoist just happens to treat B as an end—it is only accidental, in the light of A's selfishness, that B could rationally share the end of the action. There is a certain strangeness in saying that someone accidentally treats another as an end, or accidentally respects him as a person. A similar problem exists with regard to the case of the do-gooder. Given his own perspective in trying to act rightly, C treats D as a mere means by mistake. This also seems to be an undesirable consequence of Kant's view. For though one may fail to act in accordance with the principle of universality because of a mistake as to what can be a universal law, it does not seem plausible that one can violate the principle of humanity solely because of an error with regard to what can be rationally shared.

By this latter point I do not intend to suggest that what C does is right solely because he makes a strong effort to do his duty. This would be not only an absurd result of an analysis of moral judgment but also a violation of the spirit of Kant's moral philosophy. The claim I am making is more modest and limited. C's attitudes and motives, in this case making up an important part of the context of the act, are such that it is improper to charge him with treating a person merely as a means. He does respect D's rational will, and though his action may be wrong according to *some* moral standard, he is not properly condemnable on the basis of the principle of humanity. From the perspective of the second formula of the categorical imperative, the action ought to be regarded as right.

The moral judgments resulting from these applications appear to conflict with our most natural responses and most frequent intuitions in another important respect. This has to do with Kant's notion of man as a limiting condition for the adoption and pursuit of (subjective) ends. Just what is involved in making something a limiting condition or treating something as a limiting condition for actions? It is helpful to consider a different kind of case. Suppose that a child, Randolph, seeks to make his parents a limiting condition for his behavior. In order to do this, he must defer to their judgment and respect their wishes in his actions; he must do what they demand and refrain from doing what they prohibit. Being a very submissive child, Randolph makes a serious effort to behave exactly as his parents want. Unfortunately, however, he misunderstands a particular set of instructions and does not act as his parents had intended. He is consequently punished.

Another child, Ralph, is in a much different situation. He does not try to make his parents a limiting, or restrictive, condition for his conduct. Being precocious and rebellious, he even tries to act in opposition to their expressed wishes. Like Randolph, Ralph misunderstands certain imperatives issued by his parents, but in his case the combination of rebellion and miscalculation results in his behaving exactly as they really wanted him to act. He is consequently praised for being a "good boy." The situations of Randolph and Ralph parallel, respectively, those of the unfortunate do-gooder and the lucky egoist.

The examples suggest an ambiguity in the notion of a limiting condition. This ambiguity can perhaps be eliminated with the distinction between something's *being* a limiting condition and its *being treated as* a limiting condition. Randolph's conduct is not in fact limited to such actions as would be approved by his parents. Similarly, the unfortunate do-gooder's actions are not in fact within the limitations of the moral law (and thus not limited to what men can rationally share). What ought to be a limiting condition is not in fact one. Ralph's actions, however, are limited to those acceptable to his parents. And the lucky egoist's conduct is in fact restricted to the pursuit of ends which accord with the Wille of rational beings.

The situations are reversed with regard to the notion of treating something as a limiting condition. Randolph treats his parents as a limiting condition, but Ralph does not. Similarly, the unfortunate do-gooder treats the moral law, rationality, and humanity (in the person of the individual used as a means) as limiting conditions. The lucky egoist, however, treats neither men nor morality as a condition limiting his conduct. The supreme restrictions he seeks to impose on his behavior derive from the standard of his own self-interest.

The ambiguity in the notion of a limiting condition and the distinction just delineated raise an important question of interpretation. In Chapter 1 the idea of a man as a supreme limiting condition was related to the negative conception of man as an objective end for human action. It is now unclear which of the two ways of understanding this notion is applicable to the treatment of man as an end-in-himself. As we have seen, the interpretation developed in Chapter 3 (on the basis of passages from the second *Critique*) suggests that to have one's ends in fact limited by man's autonomy is both necessary and sufficient for the treatment of human beings as ends-in-themselves. Considerations have been offered, however, to support the view that this is neither necessary nor sufficient. For to *treat* man as an end appears to include at least some of what I have called internal phenomena. If a reasonable connection can be made between the treatment of persons as ends and man's status as a limiting condition, something more than merely having one's conduct accidentally limited to human autonomy appears to be required. In order to *treat* someone as an end-in-himself, the agent must treat him as a supreme condition restricting the pursuit of ends and the choice of means. But this cannot be rightly understood without reference to internal phenomena of the kind which have been discussed.

THE TREATMENT OF PERSONS AS ENDS

Must Kant's account of the principle of personality be rejected as inadequate and abandoned as unhelpful in gaining a right understanding of morality? Though no definite or conclusive solution to these problems can be obtained from the relevant texts, we need not give up hope of making Kant's view more acceptable (or, rather, of showing that it is more reasonable than it now appears to be). In order to find ways of alleviating (or at least minimizing) the difficulties, it is helpful to return to the *Groundwork*. Consider the following passages:

> Now I say that man, and in general every rational being, *exists* as an end in himself, *not merely as a means* for arbitrary use by this or that will: he must in all his actions, whether they are directed to himself or to other rational beings, always be viewed *at the same time as an end*. (*GW* 95)

> But man is not a thing—not something to be used *merely* as a means: he must always in all his actions be regarded as an end in himself. (*GW* 97)

> For then it is manifest that a violator of the rights of man intends to use the person of others merely as a means without taking into consideration that, as rational beings, they ought always at the same time to be rated as ends—that is, only as beings who must themselves be able to share in the end of the very same action. (*GW* 97)

The phrases on which we may profitably focus are "be *viewed* at the same time as an end," "be *regarded* as an end in himself," and "be *rated* as ends" (my italics). The use here of the terms 'view', 'regard', and 'rate' suggests the attitudes and beliefs of the agent.[1] These statements imply that in order to treat a person as

1. The reader may wish to consult the Academy edition of Kant's works, vol. 4, pp. 428, 430.

an end one must regard or rate him as such. If these considerations can be plausibly utilized to supplement the second *Critique* criterion, then Kant's position may perhaps escape at least one of the objections thus far brought against it.

In an attempt to understand Kant's doctrine of the end-in-itself in its entirety and to provide an interpretation which lends a maximum of consistency to his account, we may revise one significant element in the previous summary of his position. The rational sharing of morally worthwhile ends may not be sufficient for the treatment of human beings as ends-in-themselves. It may also be essential to regard or consider them in certain ways. If this is the case, the lucky egoist, as well as Schyster and Quackenbush, would not be treating people as ends-in-themselves, since they regard as mere means the persons whom they use and have no respect for them (beyond a "respect" for their ability to function as means). The fact that the aims of their actions may be morally acceptable and rationally willed would not be sufficient to make their conduct right.

Some clarifications are in order. It is important to notice that the other kind of case brought to bear against the second *Critique* position—that of the unfortunate do-gooder—is not explained by this new addition. One who tries but fails to make his purposes harmonize with the autonomy of rational agents still treats the other as a mere means (assuming, of course, that he treats him as a means at all) and thus fails to treat the other person as an end. To regard man as an end, and thus to respect him in this internal way, is not sufficient for the avoidance of treating him merely as a means. If Kant were interpreted in such a way as to make his account conform to ordinary judgment about the example, we would be forced to ignore explicit statements in both the *Groundwork* and the *Critique of Practical Reason*.

A possible difficulty with these suggestions must now be discussed. There is another way in which the remarks containing the words 'view', 'regard', and 'rate' may be understood. Kant's claim that men must be regarded as ends-in-themselves has been interpreted thus far to mean that regarding someone as an end is part of one's duty in following the principle of humanity. He may, however, mean only that we must view men as ends-in-themselves to gain a sound understanding of morality. According to such an interpretation, his position would be that any adequate moral theory must take this fact into account and must not set forth any rules or principles which do violence to man's status as an end. It is clear that Kant believes this to be true. It does not follow, however, that each man, in order to do his duty in situations in which he treats others as means, must regard, or consider, men to be ends-in-themselves. It does not follow, that is, that the *treatment* of persons as ends must of necessity involve a *regard* for them as having value (a value not limited to their usefulness as means).

A similar point may be made concerning even more technical notions in Kant's ethics. Kant is committed to the view that a sound moral theory must regard human beings as autonomous. Any ethical system whose elements in some way conflict with man's autonomy would be, to that extent, defective. It would not follow from this, however, that every moral agent would have to consider others to be autonomous in order to fulfill his moral duties. This might be an unreasonable (and perhaps even absurd) demand on people who are concerned to do what is right but who, through lack of knowledge or intelligence, are not in any position to understand the difficult notion of autonomy. Such ignorance and inability would not make them any less responsible for the fulfillment of certain moral duties; they would still have obligations to act in accordance with laws arising from the autonomous wills of rational agents. But it is one thing to act in accord with such laws and quite another to *recognize* or *regard* man as autonomous. Kant does not appear to consider the latter to be part of one's duty, despite its importance as a theoretical requirement for a sound account of moral action.

It is not fully clear whether Kant views the regarding of men as ends to be part of one's duty or merely believes it to be an essential feature of any adequate moral theory. We cannot say conclusively that in order to treat a person as an end one must view or rate him in this way. The matter is important and deserving of attention, however, because his view about it is crucial to a decision as to whether his general position can handle the previously discussed objections.

The contexts in which Kant makes the remarks containing the words 'regard' and 'rate' provide several reasons for believing that he may have viewed considering (or regarding) persons as ends as a requirement of the principle of personality. In these passages, Kant is attempting to offer sound applications of the second formulation of the categorical imperative. He provides examples of wrong action and characterizes these actions as instances of treating human beings as mere means. It seems clear that these are cases of treating people as means. But why is it alleged that the persons are treated *merely* in this way? Kant answers this question by saying, in the first example, that man "must always in all his actions be regarded as an end in himself" and, in the second, that "they ought always at the same time to be rated as ends." He appears to view the failure to regard or consider man as an end a violation of the principle of personality.

As so interpreted, Kant's position could escape at least one objection. One who regards another merely as a means (as in the case of the lucky egoist) cannot be treating him as an end, even though the latter is able to share rationally the purpose of the action. A further plausible inference is that it is not sufficient that the ends one seeks be merely restricted to morally acceptable ones or that one's purposes be limited to those which are consistent with humanity as a supreme limiting condition. In order to treat humanity as an end-in-itself, one must treat man as a supreme condition restricting the adoption and pursuit of (subjective) ends. The agent who acts in accord with the second formula will strive to seek only purposes compatible with moral laws arising from the will (Wille) of rational beings.

There is yet a further difficulty in understanding exactly what is required in order to treat man as an end. I have suggested that it would be unreasonable to demand of the ordinary man an understanding of all the technical, theoretical elements of Kantian ethics. In order to know whether the principle of humanity has been satisfied or violated, one must know what it is to regard someone as an end. On the basis of the interpretation developed in Chapter 3 and modified in the present chapter, we know what it is for man to *be* an end and also what it means for him to be *treated as* an end in a wholly external way. But this involves certain technical notions peculiar to Kantian moral theory. Man's status as an end is linked with his status as an autonomous agent, as a rational being in possession of Wille. Must every man— irrespective of his particular state of knowledge or his familiarity with these moral themes—regard, or consider, others as beings whose Wille cannot be violated and whose autonomy is to be respected? Surely not, if we are to be reasonable or just. Many persons do not even have the concepts of autonomy and rational willing, but this deficiency should not keep them from being able to satisfy the demands of the principle of personality.

There is no readily available solution to this problem. It indicates another limitation of Kant's doctrine. His view is, in this respect, not very helpful in gaining a better understanding of ordinary belief and judgment about the treatment of human beings as ends and as means. That the difficulty is a genuine one may be further demonstrated with reference to the following passages:

A rational being must always regard himself as making laws in a kingdom of ends which is possible through freedom of the will— whether it be as member or as head. (*GW* 101)

Hence the end must here be conceived, not as an end to be produced, *but as a self-existent* end. It must therefore be conceived only negatively—that is, as an end against which we should never act, and consequently as one which in all our willing we must never rate *merely* as a means, but always at the same time as an end. (*GW* 105)

In these remarks Kant appears to require too much of rational agents. (This point, it should be noted, presupposes that Kant is here delineating a duty of moral agents as opposed to a merely theoretical requirement for a sound moral theory.) The kind of technical familiarity required in order to conceive of, or regard, persons in the way described is neither possessed nor attainable by all people. The same basic point may be applied to the following claims: "For to say that in using means to every end I ought to restrict my maxim by the condition that it should also be universally valid as a law for every subject is just the same as to say this—that a subject of ends, namely, a rational being himself, must be made the ground for all maxims of action, never *merely* as a means, but as a supreme condition restricting the use of every means—that is, always also as an end" (*GW* 105). Here Kant appears to prescribe not only that persons perform actions which are in accord with man's status as a limiting condition, but also that they strive to make man this sort of condition in their decisions as to what ends and means to adopt. But, again, this notion is technical and complex. Obviously, not everyone would understand enough of what is involved in this doctrine to be in any position to consider others as such limiting conditions.

The basic problem may be summarized in the form of a dilemma: Kant's principle is either too permissive or too demanding. Interpreted as not requiring certain attitudes and motives, Kant's position has been found to be inadequate. The reasons for this are (1) that A could be understood as treating B as an end even though he regards him only as a means and (2) that C could be understood as treating D as a mere means even though he regards him as an end. Some of Kant's statements can be understood in such a way as to allow his theory to handle the first of these objections. That is, it is plausible to interpret Kant as holding that in order to treat a person as an end one must regard him as such.

But this creates a new problem. It is not clear just what is necessary in order to consider man as an end. On the basis of one plausible interpretation, Kant's position requires that one regard man as an autonomous agent, as a possessor of Wille, and as a supreme limiting condition. Yet these notions are so complex and so inaccessible to many ordinary moral agents that they may not be in a position to regard men this way. It would seem unreasonable to insist that all men treat others as ends in this sense. The duty to act in accordance with the second formulation of the categorical imperative would be an almost impossible requirement to fulfill. Thus, the changes necessary to prevent Kant's principle from being too permissive result in its being overly demanding.

There is no conclusive way of avoiding these problems. Perhaps the most reasonable approach would be to claim that regarding someone as an end does not necessitate a familiarity with the technical elements of Kant's philosophy. This may be true. But what, then, *is* required in order to regard man as an end? A danger in dealing with this question is that one's answers may very easily involve ideas markedly different from those of Kant. One may suggest, for instance, that what is required is that one have some minimal concern for the other person's interests or welfare. However plausible this may be as an analysis of the concept of man as an end-in-himself, it is not Kant's notion. This kind of answer involves a departure from his negative conception of objective ends, which is the only conception helpful in understanding his claim that one ought not to treat others merely as means.

Another possible answer is more promising. The treatment of a person as an end may require that one have respect for him and regard him as having a value that is not limited to his usefulness. This suggestion has a double advantage. It retains the general conceptions central to Kant's doctrine of the end-in-itself and at the same time conforms to our nonphilosophical, pre-analytical understanding of the duty not to treat men merely as means. It also eliminates the necessity of understanding technical notions in order to fulfill one's moral duty.

Whether Kant would regard this as an adequate interpretation cannot be determined because of the sparse, vague nature of his remarks about regarding, considering, and viewing man as an end. Even if this view is deemed acceptable, however, it would answer only one of the objections previously discussed. The case of the lucky egoist would, according to this revised interpretation, be judged in a way which is consistent with ordinary judgment: he would be treating someone merely as a means, and his action would therefore be wrong. The case of the unfortunate do-gooder would not, however, be accounted for by this modified account. A consequence of the changes suggested is that the purpose's objective agreement with rational willing is not sufficient for treating someone as as end. But such agreement and sharing are still necessary for acting rightly according to the principle of personality. Since the unfortunate do-gooder fails (even though he tries quite hard) to seek ends which can be rationally willed, he treats the other merely as a means. In this respect Kant's principle appears to conflict with ordinary moral judgment.

5 FORM AND CONTENT

The second formula arises in Kant's *Groundwork* from the expressed need to provide a content or matter for morality. The form of moral maxims is thought to be supplied by the principle of universality, but this formula requires supplementation by a principle referring to ends which are morally acceptable. The provision of these ends insures a place for the matter. Kant says:

All maxims have, in short,

1. a *form,* which consists in their universality; and in this respect the formula of the moral imperative is expressed thus: "Maxims must be chosen as if they had to hold as universal laws of nature";

2. a *matter*—that is, an end; and in this respect the formula says: "A rational being, as by his very nature an end and consequently an end in himself, must serve for every maxim as a condition limiting all merely relative and arbitrary ends";

3. a *complete determination* of all maxims by the following formula, namely: "All maxims as proceeding from our own making of law ought to harmonize with a possible kingdom of ends as a kingdom of nature." (*GW* 103–4)

In Chapter 1 it was shown why Kant believed that only something having the status of an end-in-itself could be adequate as the matter for a categorical imperative: any end without this quality could serve only as the ground of hypothetical imperatives. Only objective ends of the negative, self-existent sort are deemed acceptable, and thus, only human beings can be ends-in-themselves. On this basis, Kant concludes that in order to act rightly and therefore in accordance with the categorical imperative, one must treat human beings never merely as means but also as ends-in-themselves (*GW* 95–96).

THE CONTENT FOR MORALITY

What does it mean to treat persons as the second formulation requires? If one treats another as a means, what must he do to keep from acting wrongly? Kant's answer is that one should treat persons in such a way that they can share in the ends for whose sake they serve as means. These ends are, in one sense, subjective ones: they are purposes which can become the goals of particular actions. But what is necessary in order for someone to be able to "share" ends? The only purposes in which a person can share are those which he can, as a rational being, will. And one can rationally will only those which are morally acceptable because of their agreement with laws arising from the Wille. In this sense, the ends one must seek are objective ones. Kant's principle of humanity is thus tantamount to the following: *If one treats someone as a means, he must be seeking only morally acceptable purposes.*

This answer is somewhat disappointing. It was known at the outset of the inquiry that any ends which one pursues must be morally worthy. An adequate understanding of what Kant *calls* the matter for a categorical imperative—persons as ends-in-themselves—requires reference to what would otherwise be thought to be the matter for such imperatives—morally acceptable ends sought in human action. The principle of humanity thus appears not to supply the content for morality. Indeed, the content in the form of morally worthy ends is actually *presupposed* in Kant's statement of what it means to treat persons as ends-in-themselves.

A consequence of this unfortunate development is that in any attempt to apply the second formula, one must already know what is morally right or wrong. Suppose that Smith treats Brown as a means. In order to evaluate Smith's behavior on the basis of the principle of humanity, we must determine whether he treats Brown merely as a means. But in order to ascertain this, we must know whether the ends Smith tries to fulfill are moral ones. We must, therefore, already know something of the content of the moral law. The notion of man as an end-in-himself cannot itself supply this content. To know whether someone is treated as an end, one must know, on some basis other than the principle of humanity, what the matter of the moral law actually is.

It is no real help to say that one knows what purposes are morally acceptable on the basis of what a person can rationally will, for this was also already known on the basis of Kant's first formulation, or the principle of universality. What is apparently thought to be required is a principle going *beyond* the first formula, which presumably supplies only the form for human volition. Thus it appears that Kant has not achieved his purpose in introducing the principle of humanity. Its clarification and applicability depend on what it is itself supposed to provide. There is the paradoxical result that an application of the principle requires that what would reasonably be thought to be its own work has already been done.

A further unwelcome result is an apparent circularity in Kant's position. This can be illustrated with reference to the notion of a supreme limiting condition. This concept is an essential feature of Kant's doctrine of the end-in-itself and accounts in part for the initial plausibility of the negative conception of human beings as self-existent, objective ends. To treat man as the end-in-itself is to treat humanity as the supreme condition restricting the adoption and pursuit of means and purposes. The notion is actually a relatively simple one, as may be seen by the consideration of a very basic question.

What *does* limit or determine one's use of means? One plausible answer is this: the purposes one seeks restrict the means one adopts. In an important sense the means are dependent upon the purposes. If humanity is the supreme condition limiting the use of means, it is plausible to call man the supreme end, or the end-in-itself. In a similar fashion, man can be understood as the end-in-itself because his humanity limits the subjective purposes of actions. Persons' goals are limited (and determined) by the other ends which they seek. It is not at all unreasonable, then, to speak of the supreme limitation on all other ends as the supreme end, or the end-in-itself. The following remark, initially puzzling, can be seen to be quite natural and plausible: ". . . a subject of ends, namely, a rational being himself, must be made the ground for all maxims of action, never *merely* as a means, but as a supreme condition restricting the use of every means—that is, always also as an end" (*GW* 105). Treating men as ends is thus a way of restricting one's actions in accordance with the demands of morality.

One would probably surmise that it is on this basis that a criterion is established for determining the moral acceptability of ends. One begins with ends which people can seek to achieve. In one sense the only ends to be evaluated morally are subjective ones: they can be produced or promoted. The task is to determine which of these are also objective—that is, which are ends that ought to be sought by rational beings. In addition we may expand this positive concept of objective ends to include those which are permitted. This latter group would consist of those that do not conflict with morally required ends and principles. This general class of objective ends thus includes all ends which are morally acceptable.

But how does one determine which ends have this quality? One does so, Kant appears to believe, by measuring them against the standard provided by humanity as the end-in-itself. But here we have to utilize Kant's other basic conception of objective ends: only human beings are self-existent ends possessing absolute value. The negative conception of objective ends is morally and epistemically prior to the positive conception. In order to determine whether certain ends are morally acceptable and thus objective in the latter sense, one must know whether they are in agreement with humanity as an objctive end in the negative sense. It is only in this way that the notion of humanity as a supreme limiting condition can be made plausible.

This way of understanding the concept of humanity as an end-in-itself is vitiated by an analysis of Kant's own account of the principle of personality. In order to know whether man is treated as an end, one must know whether the purpose for which he is treated is morally acceptable. But then what ends are objective in the positive sense determines whether man is treated as an objective end in the negative sense. It is true, of course, that the moral acceptability of these ends is dependent upon whether they can be rationally shared by all men. In this way man does serve as the limiting condition for such purposes. But, again, this presupposes something which the principle itself would otherwise be expected to supply, viz., those ends which rational beings can will in accordance with the demand that their maxims be universal laws. The results of Kant's account are in this respect as well somewhat disappointing.

These points suggest that the second formula of the categorical imperative actually supplies little more than that which Kant tried to provide in his first formula. We began with the knowledge that one must be able to will (as a rational being) all actions which he contemplates performing. It advances our understanding very little to say that treating a person in such a way that he can will to be treated is to treat him as an end-in-himself. And it does not increase our knowledge of moral action to identify the latter as providing the matter, as opposed to the form, of morality.

An appropriate question at this point is this: What is the difference between matter and form with regard to these principles of morality? Kant states the form first and suggests that it is not sufficient for moral understanding. But he has analyzed the principle whose function it is to supply the matter in such a way that it is unclear how this is to be provided and how the second formula differs from the first. In one respect, this result should not be too surprising. In Kant's view, there is only one categorical imperative; the different principles are not thought of as different imperatives, or even as fundamentally different schemata for categorical imperatives, but as equivalents: "The aforesaid three ways of representing the principle of morality are at bottom merely so many formulations of precisely the same law" (*GW* 103). An argument for the equivalence of the first two formulae is contained in the following passage:

The principle "So act in relation to every rational being (both to yourself and to others) that he may at the same time count in your maxim as an end in himself" is thus at bottom the same as the principle "Act on a maxim which at the same time contains in itself its own universal validity for every rational being." For to say that in using means to every end I ought to restrict my maxim by the condition that it should also be universally valid as a law for every sub-ject is just the same as to say this—that a subject of ends, namely, a rational being himself, must be made the ground for all maxims of action, never *merely* as a means, but as a supreme condition restrict-ing the use of every means—that is, always also as an end. (*GW* 105)

Kant is not merely saying that the first two formulae mutually imply one another. Nor is he saying only that Formulations I and II are equivalent in the sense that they have the same moral im-plications, i.e., that what is right (or wrong) according to one of them will also be right (or wrong) according to the other. His claim is that the principle of personality and the principle of universality have the same meaning.

There are reasons for believing Kant to be right. Sharing ends requires that one be able rationally to will them in accordance with laws arising from one's Wille as an autonomous agent. Such laws must be universally valid maxims capable of being willed without contradiction. This latter point is not made explicit by Kant in the above argument or elsewhere in his discussion of the second formula. It can, however, be plausibly accepted on the basis of what is known about the principle of universality and about Kant's fundamental conceptions of morality and rationality. The principle of humanity—when fully analyzed and explained —appears to provide no more content than that supplied by the principle of universality.

This is not to say that either of the principles lacks content. Indeed, it might even be argued that Formulation I has more content than does the principle of humanity.[1] The correct appli-cation of the second formula is dependent upon what may be called "other moral knowledge." This other knowledge has to do with what can be rationally willed and with what ends are morally acceptable. One must know this in order to determine, in any given case, whether someone is treated merely as a means. The principle of humanity itself does not provide this information, nor does Kant, in his discussions of this formula, provide criteria for what can be in agreement with man's rational will. In the dis-cussion of the principle of universality, we are told a little more

1. This is also observed by Marcus George Singer in *Generalization in Ethics* (New York: Knopf, 1961), pp. 235–36.

than this. Kant insists that one can rationally agree only to maxims that can be willed to be universal laws. The fact that Formulation I provides more content than the second formulation is, of course, just the reverse of what we are led to believe on the basis of an initial, cursory examination of Kant's claims about the two principles.

AN ABSENCE OF EXCEPTIONS

In view of the considerations discussed in the last section, the principle of personality may be plausibly viewed as an application of the principle of universality. Let us again suppose that one has before him a case of treating a person as a means. After examining the maxim, he concludes that the action is wrong. The maxim (what Kant sometimes calls the subjective principle of an act) must involve some reference to the ends of the action. His judgment that the act is wrong is based on the belief that its subjective principle (itself based partially on what ends the agent seeks) cannot be willed to be a universal law. Since the maxim cannot be so willed, it is incompatible with laws arising from the rational will of autonomous agents. One must then conclude that the action is a case of treating a person merely as a means and thus cannot be a case of treating someone as an end-in-himself.

It is no real advance in our understanding merely to apply the phrases "treat as mere means" and "treat as ends" to actions found to be wrong and right, respectively, on these other grounds. The second formula was initially set forth as a moral principle in terms of which actions can be judged to be either permissible or prohibited. But it now appears that one must ascertain what is right or wrong *before* knowing whether any given act is an instance of treating someone as an end. This provides a very short answer to the question, What counts as an act of treating a person merely as a means? The correct reply is this: an action is a case of treating someone as a mere means if (1) it is a case of treating him as a means and (2) it is wrong. But it then becomes questionable whether it is appropriate to refer to the second formula as a moral principle. For it does not function as a criterion for determining whether certain actions are right or wrong. I am not claiming here that Kant viewed the principle as a mere application of the first formula. Though he believed them to be equivalent, he appears to have considered the second formula to be a moral principle in its own right, and not dependent upon something else. But on the basis of several of Kant's claims, it seems plausible to consider it an application of, and dependent upon, the principle of universality.

It is not wholly surprising that with Formulation II Kant offers little beyond what is provided in the discussion of the principle of universality. The negative conception of humanity as an end is based solely on man's rationality; one treats man as an end by restricting one's actions and ends to those which everyone can rationally will. But rational willing is already established in the first formulation as a supreme limiting condition. In treating man as an end, a person does what we already knew that he ought to do: he limits his conduct according to the requirements of rationality. In any case in which he fails to do this and also treats someone as a means, he will be treating that person merely as a means. To treat persons merely as a means is a way of failing to respect rational agents as concrete embodiments of rationality.

These points are related to other somewhat surprising consequences of Kant's account of the principle. He has analyzed the second formula in such a way that certain questions, otherwise perfectly plausible and deserving of answers, do not arise. In Chapter 2 several points were made about situations in which persons were thought to be able to "share" the ends for which they were treated as means. It was suggested that a person could share an end if he could benefit from its achievement or if he desired that it be realized. These examples, however, seemed also to be ones in which persons were treated as mere means. For this reason, certain interpretations of the "sharing ends" criterion were deemed inadequate, and another analysis of sharing ends was considered more plausible.

Before the shift to the "rationality" interpretation, another question might possibly have been raised. Kant says that someone is treated as a mere means because he "cannot possibly agree with my way of behaving to him, and so cannot himself share the end of the action" (*GW* 97). But what difference does this make? Why cannot a person will or agree to be treated merely as a means? Kant admits that one can treat himself merely as a means (as in the case of suicide). If he does this, could he not will to be treated this way? If he does not, why does he do it? Similarly, one individual might fully recognize that another is treating him merely as a means. Even though he has the power and the opportunity to stop the other from so acting, he does not do so. He *allows* himself to be treated merely as a means. In this case as well, can one not will that he be treated merely as a means?

The proper answer to these questions is very much like that given in reply to previous objections. What is left out of consideration is the conception of the will relevant to the notion of persons as ends-in-themselves. To treat oneself as a mere means or to be treated by another in this way cannot be in accord with the rational will (Wille). The questioner can at this point, however, pursue the matter further. Why cannot one rationally will that he be treated merely as a means? This question is very similar to another: why can it not sometimes be right for someone to be treated merely as a means? By a concentration on the right answers to these questions (from Kant's point of view), we may be better able both to understand the principle and to recognize its limitations. Kant has so used the terms "end" and "mere means" that, in virtue of the meanings he gives to certain key notions, it is logically impossible for one both to treat a person as a mere means and to act rightly.

In order to see this clearly, we may draw upon aspects of previous discussions. Kant assumes that treating a person as a mere means is incompatible with treating him as an end. Indeed, whether or not the person is treated as an end is what distinguishes cases of treating another as a mere means from those in which one is treated as a means but not only in this way. What, then, is it to treat someone as an end? The answer to this question has already been provided. To treat someone as an end is to treat him in such a way that he can rationally will the purpose of the action and rationally agree to the "way of behaving." But if one person treats another in this way, he treats him rightly. To treat a person wrongly is, on the basis of the principle of universality, to treat him in such a way that the maxim of the action cannot be willed to be a universal law. And whatever maxims can be so willed are those which one *does* will as a rational, autonomous agent in possession of Wille. These maxims are also what one *would* will if he had full control over his inclinations—if he were a completely rational being. It is logically impossible, then, both to treat someone as an end and to treat him wrongly. It is similarly impossible to treat him rightly while treating him as a mere means. Treating persons in ways which are consistent with their rational wills is just what moral action involves.

Certain questions, therefore, cannot sensibly arise. Among these are the following: Is it ever morally acceptable to treat someone as a mere means? Is it ever wrong to treat someone as a means if one is also treating him as an end? Asking such questions reflects a failure to understand what Kant means by treating persons as ends and as means. This point is again based on Kant's view that one acts rightly only if the action is in accordance with that which is dictated by the rational will. The doctrine of autonomy provides that all moral laws shall be in accord with the rational will. Otherwise, men would be expected to obey rules which they themselves had not, as rational beings, legislated. If this were so, Kant argues, men could not be free. But freedom is necessary for the very existence of morality (*DV* 22; *CPR* 89–90).

From these considerations it is clear that there can be no exceptions to the principle of humanity. Even the question, Can there be exceptions to the principle of personality? reflects an incomplete understanding of Kant's doctrine of the end-in-itself. In order to see why, it is helpful to compare this principle to other moral requirements. It cannot be viewed in the same way as, for instance, the rule against lying. One clearly may ask questions about whether it is wrong to lie and whether it is ever right to do so. One can inquire as to whether it is a sound moral rule for the guidance of human action. Even if it is found to be a rule which ought generally to be obeyed, there may be exceptions to it. Under certain conditions it may be morally permissible to lie or it may be morally wrong to tell the truth. The same kinds of considerations do not apply to the principle of humanity. For if one fully understands what Kant means by the second formula, he will not inquire about possible exceptions to it. To say that it is sometimes morally right to treat a person merely as a means would be tantamount to saying that it is sometimes morally right to act wrongly.

The basis for these claims can now be stated more fully. The point is not simply that one's rational will (Wille) will always conflict with the action under consideration. This would be true just in case (as Kant believes) it is always wrong to lie. But if the latter were the case, it would not be so because of a necessary conflict between being told a lie and being treated rightly. There is a necessary or logically inevitable conflict, however, between being treated merely as a means and being treated rightly. The basic difference between the two kinds of cases is that being told the truth is not definable in terms of rational willing, but being treated as an end means that one can rationally will the ends of the action. In virtue of the meaning of the terms, to be treated as a mere means is to be treated wrongly.[2]

These considerations suggest a further limitation on the principle. It is not very helpful in understanding our moral beliefs about treating persons as ends and as means. In what may be called the "ordinary moral understanding," there is at least the *possibility* of justified exceptions to the principle against treating persons as mere means. Questions such as those posed earlier in this section—Is it always wrong to treat persons merely as means? Ought one to treat persons as ends?—would, I believe, be regarded by most as sensible. If these questions seem odd or spurious it is probably because of a lack of clarity with regard to the key terms 'ends' and 'mere means'. Or it may be because of much moral perplexity concerning just why acting in these ways is pro-

2. Paton, "An Alleged Right to Lie," pp. 190–203; and Singer, *Generalization in Ethics,* pp. 228–33. This is not true of cases in which one is told lies. If Kant were right in his claim that lying is always wrong, it would only be the case that telling the truth is always actually found to be required by the rational will. As some have argued, Kant is probably wrong about this and very likely misapplies his own principle. But there is an important sense in which he could not be wrong in a claim that it is always wrong to treat persons as mere means. He has used the terms in such a way that this cannot sensibly be doubted.

hibited, permissible, or obligatory. But it seems unlikely that there is a logical or conceptual conflict in claims such as "It is not wrong to treat others as mere means" or "One is not morally required to treat people as ends-in-themselves."

These differences between the Kantian and the "ordinary" ways of conceiving the principle of humanity suggest difficulties in trying to use Kant's theory for solving certain moral problems. Many would, after reflection on these concepts, begin to raise some of the questions just mentioned. And if it were to turn out never to be right to treat others as mere means, we would be interested in finding out why this is so. Those elements of his theory which have thus far been considered cannot, in any very satisfactory manner, contribute in this endeavor.

Some of the concepts on which Kant focuses—respect, the absolute value of persons, human beings as limiting conditions, and autonomy—are very suggestive and do provide at least partial explanations. But what is really crucial in determining if someone is treated as a mere means is whether the end of the action is morally acceptable. If the ends for which the person is used are themselves wrong, the agent treats him merely as a means. Thus for the ordinary man to find out why violations of the principle are wrong, he must have already found out why seeking certain ends is wrong. In short, all one can discover, in the absence of an understanding of Kant's technical notions of autonomy and will, is that treating persons as mere means is wrong because one seeks morally unacceptable ends. For further enlightenment he must look elsewhere.

A SIMILARITY WITH UTILITARIANISM

In this section I shall consider a final criticism of Kant's position. Many of the moral problems involved in cases of treating people as means are not peculiar to such cases. To treat a person as a mere means is to treat him as a means to ends in which he cannot share. As we have seen, an analysis of the notion of sharing ends reveals that it means being able rationally to approve of or consent to the ends of the action. But this is a perfectly general requirement for moral action, according to

Kant's ethical theory. In *any* action which one performs, even those in which others are not treated in any way at all, the maxims and ends must be morally acceptable and thus rationally willed by everyone. For this reason, Kant's principle of humanity even appears to be superfluous.[3] It really does not matter whether a person is or is not treated as a means. The fact that the agent does this imposes on the agent no further moral obligations than those which would otherwise be expected.

Reconsideration of an earlier example may help to make this clear. Chester was said to have treated the vice-president, Mortimer, as a means to his ends of stifling labor sentiment and drumming up support for the company. He might very well have chosen other means to these goals. He might have simply made a speech calling for support and appealing to a sense of unity. For purposes of moral evaluation these two cases would be treated in the same way. In both situations the crucial question is whether Chester's purposes are morally worthwhile and thus in accord with what can be rationally willed by all men. The case in which Chester uses Mortimer as a means to these ends is really no different from the other; there is nothing about his being treated in this way that is deserving of attention *as a separate moral consideration.*

The two actions are thus either obligatory, permissible, or condemnable on grounds which have nothing crucially to do with the peculiarities of the principle against treating people as mere means. The second formula cannot function alone as a moral criterion. To apply the phrase "treatment as a mere means" to wrong actions in which persons are treated as means provides no significant advance in our understanding.

This is a most undesirable consequence. It suggests that Kant's principle cannot account for some of the clearest cases of treating others merely as means. This point can be supported and clarified by a comparison with utilitarianism. Utilitarian theories have been criticized because they can be used to justify several actions which almost everyone regards as wrong. Critics have argued that acts

3. A point somewhat similar to this is made by Atwell in "Are Kant's First Two Moral Principles Equivalent?" p. 281.

involving injustice, the breaking of promises, and even torturing people could under certain conditions lead to the greatest possible happiness or the greatest possible good. Another objection is that one might be able to achieve the greatest good for a majority of mankind by sacrificing certain individuals. In such a case one might treat these individuals as mere means to achieve the greatest happiness for the largest number of people.

An explanation of this difficulty is suggested by reflection upon the teleological character of the utilitarian theory. The emphasis is on the results of human action and on the goals which human beings ought to seek. It leaves out of account serious moral consideration of the means used in securing these ends. If it considers the significance of means at all, it does so only in what effect they have on the total amount of happiness. According to this position one should, presumably, sacrifice only the person whose death is likely to provide for the greatest good.

Many find such a theory woefully inadequate and even abhorrent. Kant's theory of morality—with its emphasis on respect, on the value of individuals, and on human dignity—appears to offer an attractive and humane alternative. One senses that these concepts are reflected in the claim that persons are to be treated as ends-in-themselves and are never to be used merely as means. It is for this reason, I suggest, that the principle is able to win such wide acceptance. But a concentration on what Kant's theory really involves reveals that what makes an action of treating a person as a means wrong is no different from what would make a similar action without such treatment wrong. The crucial factor is whether the end is morally acceptable.

In this regard, Kant's position is significantly analogous to utilitarian theories. His theory, as well as that of the utilitarians, suffers from an *overwhelming emphasis on the ends of human action*. The two theories would clash, not over this general point, but over what ends are morally acceptable and what the ultimate goal of persons' behavior should be. According to both of them, the end *does* justify the means. I do not mean to suggest that Kant's theory is no better than utilitarianism. The point is that the same kind of criticism, with respect to the treatment of persons as means, is applicable to both. It is for these reasons that

Kant's theory cannot really explain, any more than can principles of utility, our ordinary moral beliefs and judgments about the rightness or wrongness of treating people as means.

This can be seen more clearly by noting two fairly obvious examples of treating people as mere means—slavery and kidnapping. Why is slavery so severely condemned? Slavery is not considered wrong solely because it often involves a great deal of suffering. It is not objectionable simply because it may lead to the breakup of families. It is not condemnable merely because it deprives people of certain basic freedoms. It is not wrong only because the purposes sought by slave owners are usually morally unworthy and even outrageously inhumane. All of these may be legitimate grounds for moral judgments against it. But it is also considered wrong because it involves the use of human beings as mere means. And it is not at all adequate to try to account for this in terms of the wrongness of the ends for which people are used. Slavery is wrong not simply because the ends cannot be justified, but because the *means* to those purposes are reprehensible.

Similarly with kidnapping. Here again what is objectionable is something more than the ends of the kidnappers. Their actions are to be condemned because they make use of a child as a mere means. I do not wish to claim that the practices of slavery and kidnapping would be deemed morally acceptable according to Kant's theory. The point is that his account, as developed thus far, does not aid us in our own understanding of these common cases and does not explain the moral judgments we would most likely make of them. The fact that the purposes of the agent are incapable of being rationally willed is not sufficient to explain either why we believe such action to be an instance of treating someone as a mere means or why we regard it as wrong.

6 PERFECTION AND HAPPINESS

THE POSITIVE CONCEPTION OF THE END-IN-ITSELF

In the *Critique of Practical Reason* Kant develops the concept of the highest good as a union of virtue and happiness. He believes that all men have a duty to try to contribute to the realization of this value. He speaks of it as the "object" for the moral law: "The moral law commands us to make the highest possible good in a world the final object of all our conduct" (*CPR* 134). As noted in Chapter 1, Kant's search for an objective end is motivated by a desire to provide the matter, or content, for morality. This notion of the highest good is another potential candidate for the end-in-itself. Kant does not say in the *Groundwork* that the highest good is the end-in-itself. Some of his claims about it in the second *Critique,* however, are similar to his suggestions in the *Groundwork* concerning form and matter. He distinguishes the ground of the will from its object:

The moral law is the sole determining ground of the pure will. Since it is merely formal, requiring only that the form of the maxim be universally legislative, as a determining ground it abstracts from all material and thus from every object of volition. Consequently, though the highest good may be the entire *object* of a pure practical reason, *i.e.,* of a pure will, it is still not to be taken as the *determining ground* of the pure will. (*CPR* 113)

In view of this and other passages it might be persuasively argued that the highest good is most plausibly regarded as the end-in-itself. I do not propose to concern myself directly with the numerous complexities involved in that notion; this would take the present project far beyound its more modest aims.[1] The main effort thus far has been to examine the Kantian principle prohibiting the treatment of persons as mere means. The concept of the end-in-itself is relevant primarily because of the contrasts between acting in this way and treating persons as ends. Nowhere, however, does Kant contrast treating men as mere means with seeking to bring about the highest good. Instead of extensively discussing the concept of the highest good, I shall consider two duties which appear to constitute at least a partial basis for it.

Kant holds that one has duties to seek his own perfection and to bring about the happiness of others. The most extensive discussion of these "ends which are also duties" is in the second part of the *Metaphysics of Morals*. There Kant attempts to establish them as "imperfect" obligations shared by all men. In the *Groundwork* Kant devotes attention to these duties in two of his sample applications of the categorical imperative; here, he attempts to link them directly and specifically with treating man as an end-in-himself. I shall be principally concerned with these connections and with this way of characterizing the duties. An effort will be made to examine their plausibility as part of a correct understanding of the notion of man as an end. Further, I shall inquire whether they are helpful in developing our understanding of why it is wrong to treat men merely as means.

It is important to take note of a few more preliminary matters. I claimed in Chapter 1 that Kant wanted to establish what he calls an "objective end" for the moral law. This was deemed necessary in order to provide an object for a categorical imperative, as opposed to a merely hypothetical one. I also argued that Kant has two different conceptions of objective ends. The essentially negative conception has been emphasized thus far, because it is relevant to cases of treating men as means and to the notion

1. On the highest good, see the following articles by John R. Silber: "Kant's Conception of the Highest Good as Immanent and Transcendent," *Philosophical Review* 68 (1959): 469–92; "The Metaphysical Importance of the Highest Good as the Canon of Pure Reason in Kant's Philosophy," *Texas Studies in Literature and Language* 1 (1959): 233–44; "The Importance of the Highest Good in Kant's Ethics," *Ethics* 73, no. 3 (April 1963): 179–97.

of sharing ends. In this negative sense, an objective end is what Kant calls "self-existent," or "already existent." It is to serve as the supreme limiting condition of all ends that can be produced as the results of actions; it is not the sort of end which can itself be produced. On this basis, Kant argues that man alone can be an objective end and claims that man is the end-in-itself for morality.

In the third and fourth illustrations in the *Groundwork* man becomes an end-in-itself in quite a different sense. We are told that in order to treat men as ends-in-themselves, we must seek our own perfection and the happiness of others. In this discussion the positive conception of objective ends emerges. In this sense, objective ends are those which men ought to seek as their purposes in action. Here the notion of an "end" appears to be the same as our ordinary concept of an end—that is, a purpose of an action or way of life. While some of Kant's earlier remarks seem to exclude this sort of end as a viable candidate for the end-in-itself—he explicitly rejects at one point ends which can be produced (*GW* 105)— nonetheless, objective ends in this positive sense do have an important place in Kant's doctrine of the end-in-itself.

It may be difficult to conceive of man as an objective end in this positive sense. What sense does it make to talk of seeking as an end man himself—the sort of entity which, as Kant points out, is already in existence? Yet Kant clearly does consider human beings to be objective ends both negatively and positively. Treating man as an end in the negative sense is not sufficient for the performance of one's duty; one must also make humanity the end of his actions by seeking to develop his own perfection and by trying to advance the happiness of others. It is in this way that these duties are linked with the treatment of human beings as ends-in-themselves.

The duties of perfection and happiness are only imperfect obligations. In part, this means that they are not "determinate"— that is, what is required to fulfill them is not completely specified. In contrast, the first two sample applications (suicide and the false promise) provide examples of perfect obligations. One has a perfect, or strict, duty not to treat himself or others as mere means. If one treats someone as a means, he has a perfect, or absolute, obligation to treat him, at the same time, as an end-in-himself. Within this negative conception of man as an end, no latitude is given to the agent to determine when he will treat others as ends-in-themselves. If in any situation he treats someone merely as a means, he has acted wrongly.

The duties to seek perfection and happiness are less stringent. There are many situations in which one may have the opportunity to make himself better or to further others' happiness. To fail to do so, however, is not to violate one's duty to treat man as an end in the positive sense. The agent is granted a considerable degree of latitude within which to decide how to go about fulfilling his imperfect duties. He is left free to decide when he will develop his talents and which of these he will cultivate. He is allowed to determine for himself when he will seek others' happiness and whose he will try to advance. These duties are indeterminate because they are described in such a way that one can obtain no clear idea of exactly what is required in order to fulfill his obligations.

The treatment of man as an end-in-itself in the positive sense is thus not an absolute, or strict, requirement of the moral law. As paradoxical as it may seem, one is not always required to treat human beings as ends. To fail to do so on some particular occasion is not to transgress a moral requirement. For this and other reasons, the positive conception is not very useful for understanding the prohibition against treating people as mere means. In one respect, however, the positive conception is helpful. It does supply part of the content for morality: we are given two examples of ends morally required as objects of the moral law.

ONE'S OWN PERFECTION AS A DUTY

In the introduction to the *Doctrine of Virtue* Kant speaks of objective ends in the following way: "The doctrine of Law deals only with the *formal* conditions of outer freedom (the consistency of outer freedom with itself if its maxim were made universal law)—that is, with <u>Law</u>. But ethics goes beyond this and provides a *matter* (an object of free choice), an end of pure reason which it presents also as an objectively necessary end, *i.e.,* an end which, so far as men are concerned, it is a duty to have" (*DV* 38). The first of these objectively necessary ends, perfection, has two components. Natural perfection consists in the cultivation of talents and the development of natural abilities. Moral perfection involves striving to become more virtuous, and thus, to become a better person according to the requirements of the moral law. To seek to develop oneself in both ways is an integral element of treating oneself as an end. In order to recognize the plausibility of this idea, it is helpful to consider exactly what Kant says about perfection in the *Groundwork*:

> . . . in regard to contingent (meritorious) duty to oneself, it is not enough that an action should refrain from conflicting with humanity in our own person as an end in itself: it must also *harmonize with this end*. Now there are in humanity capacities for greater perfection which form part of nature's purpose for humanity in our person. To neglect these can admittedly be compatible with the *maintenance* of humanity as an end in itself, but not with the *promotion* of this end. (*GW* 97–98)

The conception of humanity as an end relevant to this passage is the positive one. Merely to refrain from acting contrary to man's status as an end-in-himself is not sufficient for the fulfillment of one's duty. One must also treat oneself as an end in a more positive sense: each individual must promote or further humanity in his own person by developing certain qualities.

A key concept for this discussion is the notion of development. I have already noted certain conceptual difficulties in the idea of man as an end: an end is generally thought to be a purpose that can be brought about through action, and human beings do not appear to be entities which fit this general description. These difficulties seem to have been partially responsible for Kant's claim that human beings are ends of such a peculiar sort—self-existent ones. The notion of development, however, can render more acceptable a claim that human beings can be ends in the ordinary sense. Kant insists that in order to treat oneself as an end in the positive sense, one must strive to develop capacities for greater perfection. By seeking a goal roughly describable as "one's own development," one makes of himself an end of his actions.

Humanity becomes an end, then, insofar as one's personal development becomes an end which one seeks to attain.

With the introduction of these ideas, Kant is no longer insistent that man be an end solely in the sense of a negative, self-existent, limiting condition for actions and purposes. Perfection is an objective end in the sense that it should be sought by all human beings (and presumably, by every rational agent who is not wholly or necessarily rational). But seeking perfection as a goal is also a way of treating humanity itself as an objective end. Humanity thus becomes an objective end in the positive as well as in the negative sense.

This, unfortunately, is in direct conflict with some of Kant's explicit claims about man as an end-in-himself. Consider the following passage:

> Rational nature separates itself out from all other things by the fact that it sets itself an end. An end would thus be the matter of every good will. But in the Idea of a will which is absolutely good—good without any qualifying condition (namely, that it should attain this or that end)—there must be complete abstraction from every end that has to be *produced* (as something which would make every will only relatively good). Hence the end must here be conceived, not as an end to be produced, *but as a self-existent* end. It must therefore be conceived only negatively—that is, as an end against which we should never act, and consequently as one which in all our willing we must never rate *merely* as a means, but always at the same time as an end. (*GW* 105)

Here, Kant expressly eliminates from consideration as plausible candidates for objective ends all ends that can be produced or promoted. I know of no way of resolving this conflict in Kant's doctrine of the end-in-itself. It can be explained, however, as a result of the need to accommodate divergent elements in the system. On the one hand, man is said to be an end only in the negative sense of a self-existent limiting condition because of Kant's belief that only such ends are suitable for categorical imperatives (as opposed to merely hypothetical ones). On the other hand, some positive notion is necessary in order to make the second formula commensurate with all four sample applications of the categorical imperative.

In his discussion of the principle of universality Kant provides examples which involve imperfect moral duties. The duties derived have to do with developing one's own personal capacities and with contributing to the well-being of those in need. He is committed, however, to the view that all of the various formulae of the categorical imperative are equivalent. If they are equivalent they must have the same moral implications; they must apply in the same ways to the same situations. If a particular duty is derivable on the basis of the principle of universality, it must also be deducible from the principle of personality. It is necessary to show the applicability of the second formula to all the cases used for illustrating the first principle.

The negative duties regarding suicide and the false promise can be explained, Kant thinks, as cases of treating people as mere means. On the basis of the logical or conceptual connections between treating people as ends and treating them as means, the agent fails to treat another as an end-in-himself and therefore acts wrongly. Kant is able to make this point while keeping to the negative conception of humanity as a self-existent end serving as a supreme limiting condition. But the duties regarding perfection and happiness are not, at least in any clearly plausible way, amenable to such an analysis. They are imperfect duties which do not bind men strictly, or absolutely, and are not, in any direct way, tied to the general obligation not to treat human beings as mere means. Not surprisingly, a different concept of man as an end is essential in order to bring these obligations under the requirements of the principle of humanity.

Thus, despite its integral role in Kant's formulations of the principle and its importance as a basic feature of the doctrine of the end-in-itself, the notion of treating persons as mere means drops out of consideration in the discussion of the third and fourth examples. Some other kind of argument must be provided in order to show that seeking perfection and happiness is a way of treating people as ends. Consider this passage from the *Doctrine of Virtue:*

> *Natural* perfection is *cultivation* of all one's *powers* for promoting the ends that reason puts forward. That natural perfection is a duty and so an end in itself, and that the cultivation of our powers even

without regard for the advantage it brings has an unconditioned (moral) imperative rather than a conditioned (pragmatic) one as its basis, can be shown in this way. The power to set an end—any end whatsoever—is the characteristic of humanity (as distinguished from animality). Hence there is also bound up with the end of humanity in our own person the rational will, and so the duty, to make ourselves worthy of humanity by culture in general, by procuring or promoting the *power* to realize all possible ends, so far as this power is to be found in man himself. In other words, man has a duty to cultivate the crude dispositions in human nature by which the animal first raises itself to man. To promote one's natural perfection is, accordingly, a duty in itself. (*DV* 51)

The duty to treat man as an end is linked with a duty to further certain capacities which distinguish human beings from other phenomena. A central and distinctive feature of human nature is, in Kant's view, the power to set ends and to realize them. Insofar as one tries to cultivate these abilities, he develops himself as a human being. Humanity in one's own person, as an object of development or improvement, thus becomes an end. By developing his powers to realize purposes, one acts out of respect for his own rationality. The reason for this is that the ability to set ends and to seek them *as purposes* (rather than merely to do things which lead to certain *results*) is a mark of rationality.

It is important to note the way Kant uses the term 'reason'. The notion of rationality operative in this context is a morally neutral one. Kant says that one has a duty to try to cultivate those powers necessary to realize "all possible ends." These goals are not limited to those which would be deemed morally acceptable or objective. In one sense of 'rationality' a man is rational only insofar as he adopts and seeks morally worthy purposes. In another, however, every human being is always—regardless of the particular state of his moral development—a rational being. His being rational in this way is partially due to his capacity for adopting and seeking ends. It is in this latter sense of 'rationality' that the duty to cultivate natural powers is linked to respect for one's rationality as a human being.

A serious consequence of this position is that one could cultivate his powers, and thus treat himself as an end, even though he does so in order to realize purposes which are morally bad. The net result of one's fulfillment of this imperfect duty might be that more wrong actions are performed than right ones. (Perhaps a supreme example of virtue would be a situation in which one has the ability to realize all of the ends set before him but has the will or moral strength to resist the morally objectionable ones.) Another possibility is that one could treat himself as a mere means in the course of trying to advance his natural perfection. A person could cultivate certain natural powers or talents in order to be better able to make use of himself as a means, but as I have already indicated, the ends toward which he strives could quite possibly be bad ones. If so, they could not be in accord with the rational will of moral agents. In such a case one would be treating himself merely as a means and would be violating his duty to treat his own humanity as an end-in-itself (in the negative sense). In one and the same situation, then, one could treat himself as an end positively but fail to do so negatively.

Is Kant's doctrine of the end-in-itself incoherent? To resolve this seeming inconsistency, we must consider further Kant's distinction between perfect and imperfect duties. I have noted that while perfect duties bind persons in a strict way, imperfect ones allow a certain degree of latitude to the agent to decide for himself when and in what way he will fulfill them. This is, of course, quite reasonable. Otherwise one would, whenever he had the opportunity, always be required to be cultivating his talents or to be striving to make others happy. This would result in a kind of moral fanaticism in anyone who conscientiously attempted to act in accordance with such requirements. One would be placed under absurd and ethically ridiculous demands. Not only would he have no time to pursue his own interests, but he would be forced to neglect a large number of more important moral duties. Kant obviously would not countenance this sort of conflict in the moral life. Granting latitude with regard to the duties of perfection and happiness may perhaps be viewed as a gesture of generosity to human beings already burdened with difficulties involved in acting rightly.

There is another element in the notion of an imperfect duty which we must consider. Perfect duties bind moral agents in such a way that the failure to perform them—in any situation in which one is faced with the opportunity—is to act wrongly. Though imperfect duties do not in this way restrict one's conduct, the latitude which they allow also involves certain restrictive features. One's performance of the duty to cultivate his own natural perfection must be limited by the constraints of other duties which he also possesses. Someone could cultivate his natural physical talents by stealing someone else's athletic equipment. Or one could develop his intellectual gifts by lying about his academic background in order to get accepted at a good university. In such situations the person would, according to Kant, be acting wrongly. He could not justify his actions on the ground that he is simply trying to fulfill his obligation to treat himself as an end by advancing his natural perfection. In this way as well, the duty to cultivate one's natural powers is an imperfect one.

Such considerations may now be applied to the case in which a person develops his powers for bad ends and treats himself merely as a means. It is *always* wrong to treat either oneself or someone else as a mere means. If someone could develop his natural talents only by treating himself as a mere means, he would have to defer until another occasion this form of personal advancement. In such a case one would have a duty not to develop his natural talents and thus would have an obligation *not* to treat himself as an end.

These developments suggest the need for a reformulation of the principle of personality. The original formulation is "Act in such a way that you always treat humanity, whether in your own person or in the person of any other, never simply as a means, but always at the same time as an end" (*GW* 96). This statement of the principle should be limited only to the negative conception of man as a supreme limiting condition. The positive conception (of man as an end to be sought) requires some such formulation as follows: "Act in such a way that you treat humanity, whether in your own person or in the person of any other, as an end— except in circumstances such that doing so would also involve the treatment of people merely as means, or would involve the violation of any perfect duty required by the moral law." The provision of this formulation alters the picture one usually gets from

Kant's claims about the principle of humanity. What Kant says leads us to regard the treatment of persons as ends as a form of conduct which goes beyond and compensates for the treatment of them as means. For this reason, treating people as ends appears to be a safe way of avoiding the treatment of them as mere means. We now find, however, that treating someone as an end may result in the treatment of him as a mere means. It must, then, sometimes be disallowed.

Kant's claims about moral perfection are not entirely amenable to this type of analysis. He believes that we have an obligation to seek the *"cultivation of morality* in us," and that "man's greatest moral perfection is to do his duty and this *from a motive of duty* (to make the law not merely the rule but also the motive of his actions)" (*DV* 52). Each person's duty is to *strive* to advance his moral perfection; one does not have an obligation actually to attain it. He says: "Hence this duty too—the duty of valuing the worth of one's actions not merely by their legality but also by their morality (our attitude of will)—is of only wide obligation. The law does not prescribe this inner action in the human mind itself but only the maxim of the action: the maxim of striving with all one's might to make the thought of duty for its own sake the sufficient motive of every dutiful action" (*DV* 53). To treat oneself as an end involves trying to become a better person—striving to develop a good will. One must try to determine what his duty is, attempt to act in accordance with it, and strive to make the dutiful character of the action his determinate motive. Kant contrasts an action's being in accordance with duty with its being done out of respect for the moral law by the use of the terms 'legality' and 'morality'. Mere legality is insufficient for the moral worth of an action.

In these passages Kant appears to alter somewhat the distinction made in the *Groundwork* between moral rightness and moral worth. Moral rightness can no longer simply be identified with being in accordance with duty. Now Kant sets forth a *duty* to strive for moral worth, to strive to make respect for duty a sufficient reason for one's actions. But the original distinction retains some of its force because of the imperfect character of the duty of moral perfection. One does not necessarily violate a duty or do something wrong when he fails to act from the proper motive. The duty is imperfect for a reason different from those underlying other imperfect duties. The point is not that one must be allowed to choose when and under what conditions he will have a good motive for his dutiful action. Every person must always try to make his actions have moral worth. The essential consideration in characterizing the duty as imperfect is that it would otherwise be too burdensome and nearly impossible to fulfill. For one cannot know the real motives for much of his conduct:

> For man cannot so scrutinize the depths of his own heart as to be quite certain, in even a single action, of the purity of his moral purpose and the sincerity of his attitude, even if he has no doubt about the legality of the action. Very often he mistakes his own weakness, which counsels him against the venture of a misdeed, for virtue (which is the notion of strength); and how many people who have lived long and guiltless lives may not be merely *fortunate* in having escaped so many temptations? It remains hidden from the agent himself how much pure moral content there has been in the motive of each action. (*DV* 52)

Kant thus bases the imperfect quality of the duty on certain inevitable limitations of self-knowledge.[2]

How does this duty relate to the treatment of persons merely as means? I have claimed that one could treat himself as an end in seeking his natural perfection even though he also treats himself merely as a means. This is based on the fact that the ends for the sake of which one wishes to cultivate his natural powers may be morally objectionable. Can some similar point be made about moral perfection? Moral perfection consists of doing one's duty from the motive of duty. One does not have an obligation to achieve such a state of virtue, but he does have a duty to strive for it. Let us suppose that someone does in this way treat himself as an end. Could he also treat himself merely as a means? I believe that he can. Suppose that he treats himself as a means. In order to keep from acting wrongly according to the negative conception of the second formula, all of his ends must be capable

---

2. On this and related points see Paul Dietrichson, "What Does Kant Mean by 'Acting from Duty'?," in *Kant,* ed. Wolff, pp. 314–30.

of being rationally willed by rational beings. But in this case the agent is mistaken about what ends are morally acceptable. He believes that the end for which he makes himself a means is rationally willed when in fact it is not. And he believes himself to be acting out of respect for the moral law, and out of respect for himself as a rational agent, even though his deep motivation is to advance his own happiness through the treatment of himself as a means. Furthermore, the ends which would make him happy might very well be ones that ought morally to be avoided. The person would, then, at the same time strive to advance his own perfection and treat himself as a mere means. One would be treating himself in this way in those situations in which he fails actually to advance his perfection.

In such a case one would be treating himself as an end in a positive way but would fail to do so in the negative sense. If Kant had classified the duty of perfection as a perfect one, there would be no possibility of such a conflict. For then if one treated himself as an end through fulfilling the duty of perfection, the ends actually sought would be morally acceptable and would be sought for worthy reasons. If such were the case, there would be no possibility (in this sort of situation) of treating persons as mere means. Kant's requirement, however, is only that one strive to be virtuous. Insofar as an individual does this, he treats himself as an end in the positive sense. It is this limited nature of the duty of perfection which makes it imperfect. The duty of treating people as ends in the negative sense actually requires much more of the moral agent. This point should also serve to alter the impression that the fulfillment of imperfect duties involves going beyond the requirements of perfect ones. The fact that one satisfies the demands imposed by the imperfect duty to treat oneself as an end does not insure the fulfillment of the perfect duty to treat oneself this way. Kant's claim that "it is not enough that an action should refrain from conflicting with humanity in our own person as an end in itself: it must also *harmonize with this end*" (*GW* 97) is somewhat misleading. Taking all of his claims into account, we can see that neither of these is "enough."

It is therefore appropriate to offer another reformulation of the principle of personality in order to make clear what it requires:

"One ought not to treat himself or others merely as means even if he treats himself as an end through seeking moral perfection." The purpose of these reformulations is to make clearer the relationships between the treatment of human beings as means and the several ways in which they may be treated as ends. Unfortunately, Kant does not always make these connections explicit. The variety of elements to be accommodated within his system results in a complexity in the doctrine of the end-in-itself which is not evident on the basis of his own statements about the principle of personality.

Let us summarize, then, the connection between the fulfillment of the duty of perfection and the treatment of oneself as an end. Kant speaks somewhat vaguely of "capacities for greater perfection which form part of nature's purpose for humanity in our person" (*GW* 97–98). "Nature's purpose for humanity" would appear to include the fulfillment of all ends which wholly rational beings would choose. These rational ends are appropriate in view of the nature of rational beings. In seeking his own moral perfection a person would be acting in accordance with his very nature as an individual who, although he possess desires or inclinations, is a rational agent. The effort to attain rational ends out of respect for duty would thus represent a striving for a fuller realization of one's nature as a human being, for a more complete realization of one's humanity.

Humanity, or human nature, thus becomes an end which can be adopted and sought in action. It is obvious, of course, that a failure to treat oneself as an end does not make one any less human. The point, rather, is that in becoming more rational and virtuous one becomes more of what a person can and should be. In this development of the distinctive qualities of human beings and in the enhancement of characteristics distinguishing them from other phenomena, humanity becomes an end-in-itself in the positive sense, not merely a negative, self-existent supreme limiting condition.

In the following passage Kant explicity affirms that humanity must become an end for the will and for action: "The first principle of the doctrine of virtue is: act according to a maxim of *ends* which it can be a universal law for everyone to have.—According to this principle man is an end, to himself as well as to others. And it is not enough that he has no title to use either himself or others merely as means (since according to this he can still be indifferent to them): it is in itself his duty to make man as such his end" (*DV* 55–56). Kant uses the word 'end' here in very much the same way as it is ordinarily employed and understood. Humanity is an end that all persons ought to adopt, and it is the sort of end that can be promoted through rational willing and moral action. Striving for virtue in one's own person is one way of promoting it.

OTHERS' HAPPINESS AS AN OBJECTIVE END

The principle of personality is quite demanding. It requires that persons not be treated merely as means. It also commands that one seek to procure his own natural and moral development by setting perfection as one of his aims. It might be thought that this is quite enough for a single principle to impose on moral agents. In Kant's view, however, still more is required. Fulfillment of the duty to treat persons as ends must also involve an effort to advance their happiness. This idea is introduced in the following passage:

. . . as regards meritorious duties to others, the natural end which all men seek is their own happiness. Now humanity could no doubt subsist if everybody contributed nothing to the happiness of others but at the same time refrained from deliberately impairing their happiness. This is, however, merely to agree negatively and not positively with *humanity as an end in itself* unless every one endeavours also, so far as in him lies, to further the ends of others. For the ends of a subject who is an end in himself must, if this conception is to have its *full* effect in me, be also, as far as possible, *my* ends. (*GW* 98)

Before we consider arguments for this duty, it is important to note some of its general characteristics. Like the duty of perfection, the obligation to seek others' happiness is only an imperfect one. Kant does not require that one always further others' happiness, so that if a person has the opportunity to make someone happy but chooses not to do so, he has not necessarily violated a requirement of the moral law. The agent is granted the latitude to decide for himself, within limits which themselves cannot be determinately specified, whom he will make happy and when he will do so.

Another basic feature of this duty is that it is an obligation one owes others. It does not apply to one's efforts to satisfy his own inclinations and to secure his own self-interest. As noted in the first chapter, Kant believes that each man naturally seeks his own happiness. He even appears to believe that, subject to certain qualifications, one cannot help but seek his own welfare. There would thus be no point in specifying a duty to oneself to try to achieve one's own happiness.³ In this respect men already treat themselves as ends.

In the paragraph quoted above Kant characterizes this imperfect duty in at least two ways. Thus far I have referred to it as an obligation to seek others' *happiness*. But Kant also says that one must try to further others' *ends*. An obvious problem with this way of stating the requirement is that many purposes are morally unacceptable, and to seek to fulfill such ends is one way of acting wrongly. It is thus conceivable that in treating others as ends by seeking to achieve their purposes (making the ends of others one's own), one could be performing a wrong action. Furthermore, in such a situation one might even be seeking to fulfill someone's bad purpose by treating either oneself or another as a means. One would then—because the ends of the action are not in accordance with the rational will—be treating someone merely as a means. In treating people as ends in the positive sense, then, one could violate the duty to treat them as ends in the negative way. In order to eliminate these problems, we must qualify the claim that one ought to make the ends of others one's own. A rough characterization of the duty would be as follows: "One ought to treat persons as ends by seeking to fulfill their purposes,

3. It should be noted that Kant's account on this point is not always consistent. He says, for example, that "to assure one's own happiness is a duty (at least indirectly); for discontent with one's state, in a press of cares and amidst unsatisfied wants, might easily become a great *temptation to the transgression of duty*" (*GW* 67). Here, Kant appears to regard the satisfaction of one's own desires as a value only as a means to the performance of duty. The happiness of others, however, is an end-in-itself.

except in situations in which their aims are morally unacceptable." But there are other difficulties. We are required, Kant says, to seek to further the happiness of others. One reasonable way of doing this is to adopt the ends of others as one's own. But the achievement of someone's purposes may not always be conducive to the furtherance of his happiness. Let us suppose that Kant is right in the claim that each man by nature seeks his own welfare or happiness. Believing that some particular object will make him happy A sets about to acquire it. He is mistaken about this, however, for achieving the goal makes him very unhappy. The intermediate ends, the achievement of which was thought likely to produce happiness, do not have their intended result. If someone else, B, had known of A's purposes, he might have sought to help him fulfill them on the ground that he has a duty to treat other people as ends. Let us suppose that B does not desire to make A happy and that he knows that these ends will lead only to unhappiness. Does he treat A as an end?

The two characterizations within Kant's discussion lead to different answers to this question. Since B does not try to procure A's happiness, we may conclude that B does not treat A as an end. But given Kant's remarks about seeking the ends of others, we could conclude that B *does* treat A as an end. What may have led Kant to make statements having these incompatible implications is the relatively strong correlation which may obtain between the pursuit of happiness and the pursuit of intermediate ends leading to happiness. But Kant also recognizes a serious difficulty in determining what will make someone happy. He even suggests that this problem is virtually insoluble (*GW* 85–86). The elimination of the conflict requires a reformulation of the duty roughly as follows: "One ought to treat persons as ends by trying to achieve their purposes when doing so would, to the best of one's knowledge, lead to their happiness."

But why does one have a duty to make others happy? And how is the advancement of their welfare related to the treatment of human beings as ends? In the following passage from the *Metaphysics of Morals* Kant presents an argument for this imperfect duty to others:

Our *well-wishing* can be unlimited, since in it we need do nothing. But *doing good* to others is harder, especially if we should do it from duty, at the cost of sacrificing and mortifying many of our desires, rather than from inclination (love) toward others.—The proof that beneficence is a duty follows from the fact that our self-love cannot be divorced from our need of being loved by others (*i.e.*, of receiving help from them when we are in need), so that we make ourselves an end for others. Now our maxim cannot be obligatory [for others] unless it qualifies as a universal law and so contains the will to make other men our ends too. The happiness of others is, therefore, an end which is also a duty. (*DV* 53)

In this argument there appears to be a discrepancy between Kant's premises and his conclusion. In the statement of the premises he writes of persons who are "in need" and require "help." The conclusion is much broader, for it is stated in terms of others' happiness. Helping someone who is in need may, of course, result in greater happiness for him. But on the other hand, it may not actually increase his happiness—even in cases in which it diminishes or eliminates his unhappiness. In addition, one may have many opportunities to increase someone else's happiness in situations in which the person made happier is not really in need. Giving certain people large amounts of money, for instance, may make them happier even though they have much already, so much that it would be incorrect to say that they "need" any more.

Since Kant's conclusion is stated so broadly, we may assume that the duty does not apply solely to situations in which others need help. He says that the happiness of others is an "end which is also a duty" and refers to it as "obligatory end" (*DV* 53). It may be fulfilled in a wide variety of situations, and one presumably would not fulfill this responsibility if he were to limit his efforts to make others happy solely to situations in which someone requires assistance. This cannot, however, be stated definitely and without qualification. The indeterminate character of the obligation as an imperfect duty precludes a clear and specific account of any exact requirements. How a particular individual fulfills the duty will depend upon his own resources, inclinations, and opportunities.

Kant's argument for this duty is based on the claim that each man by nature wills his own happiness. He insists that we treat ourselves as ends in this way. Furthermore, the desire for happiness results in our making ourselves ends *for others*: we will that others seek our happiness. In other words, we desire that our ends (which will result in our happiness) become their ends. We thus will that others treat us as ends-in-themselves in this positive sense. Are we justified in willing (and acting upon) the maxim that others treat us this way?

At this point Kant brings the universalization requirement into the discussion. According to the principle of universality, the only acceptable maxims are those that can be willed to be universal laws. As it stands, the above maxim is not yet universalized. In order to be truly universal, it must be modifed so as to include the happiness of others. A person could not be willing for everyone else to act on the maxim allowing each to seek his own happiness exclusively. But if a person wills that others adopt a maxim providing for *his* happiness, then he must, in order to avoid a "contradiction in his will," adopt a maxim providing for *their* happiness. If one tries to will that the happiness of human beings not be sought, he cannot do so without going against his will that his own happiness be made an end of others.[4]

The duty to treat others as ends-in-themselves is thus based on an individual's self-interested desire for his own happiness; indeed, the argument is actually dependent upon the fact that all persons, by virtue of their nature as sensible beings, have this desire. If one did not will his own well-being or happiness, he would presumably have no duty to treat others as ends-in-themselves (in the positive sense). The status of human beings as positive ends-in-themselves is thus conditioned in a way in which their status as ends in the negative sense of supreme limiting conditions is not.

It is appropriate to recall an argument discussed in Chapter 1. Kant claims that men are ends-in-themselves by virtue of their nature as rational agents. In that argument he says that each man of necessity conceives of himself as an end. The conclusion of the argument, however, is not dependent upon this fact. For given the conception of human beings as ends relevant in that context,

4. Cf. Julius Ebbinghaus, "Interpretation and Misinterpretation of the Categorical Imperative," in *Kant,* ed. Wolff, pp. 224–26.

all men are to be treated as ends-in-themselves regardless of whether anyone conceives of them as such. The duty to treat others as ends is not based on the necessity of universalization beyond one's own case (*GW* 96). The differences between the two conceptions of persons as objective ends thus lead to two different ways of arguing for duties based on the second formula. Kant's concept of human nature is crucial to both arguments. Rationality is emphasized in the development of the negative conception, while sensibility plays a central role in the accounts involving the positive conception.

But why is making others happy thought to be a way of treating them as ends? In the previous section I suggested that advancing toward perfection could be understood as the realization of human nature, as the development of that of which human beings are capable. Human beings would thus be made the ends of actions insofar as their own development becomes an end of willing and acting. It seemed reasonable to characterize the duty of perfection as a way of realizing human nature because it was understood as the realization of distinctively human capacities: in improving moral character, one enhances those qualities which, in Kant's view, distinguish human beings from other animals and from inanimate phenomena. But man's natural end of happiness is, presumably, something which he shares with other animals. Happiness, it will be recalled, is importantly related to inclinations. Kant does not offer an explicit account of the exact connection between the satisfaction of inclinations and the advancement of happiness, but in order to determine what will make any particular individual happy, one must consider what that person actually desires. If happiness can be roughly characterized as the satisfaction of inclinations, then both man and the lower animals can be happy or unhappy. The furtherance of happiness cannot rightly be understood as the realization of some distinctively *human* potentiality.

The realization of human nature has thus far been characterized as the development of those capacities which differentiate human beings from the lower animals. On the basis of this conception, the imperfect duty to further the happiness of others cannot be understood as an obligation involving the realization of human nature. If so, what sense does it make to speak of the performance of this duty as a way of treating persons as ends? In order to make Kant's view more plausible, it is necessary to broaden this account of what it is to "realize human nature."

Sensibility is just as much a part of human nature as rationality. Having inclinations, or desires, is essential to being human despite the fact that other creatures also possess them. Kant appears to hold that it is human nature for men to seek their happiness or to try to satisfy their inclinations. Indeed, this quality is one component which makes man a moral agent. His possession of inclinations makes it probable that he will sometimes be tempted to act wrongly, while the possession of rationality provides his responsibility for acting in accordance with the moral law and thus insures that he will have duties. If man were either necessarily rational or wholly sensible (merely phenomenal), he could not have obligations and could not be a moral agent.

Thus, seeking the happiness of others may be understood as a way of acting in accordance with their nature as human beings. In acting for the sake of others' happiness one acts for the sake of *man* and may have humanity itself as an end. As with the duty of perfection, the duty of happiness involves the notion of man as an end actually to be realized in human action, not as a supreme limiting condition. It is an end to be promoted or produced. In this respect Kant's view diverges from his claims in the passages in which he introduces the principle of personality. His doctrine apparently had to be adjusted in order to make the principle apply to imperfect duties as well as perfect ones. With this concept of man as an end, Kant provides some of the content for the moral law and for human volition. Perfection and happiness are ends which also are duties, and fulfilling them is tantamount to the treatment of man himself as an end.

But how does the performance of these duties relate to the treatment of persons as mere means? Kant's way of introducing the positive obligation in the *Groundwork* makes it appear that acting in accordance with this requirement goes beyond merely refraining from treating people in this way (*GW* 98). This is entirely consistent with the subsequent development of his position in the *Metaphysics of Morals*. It should be clear, however, that one can be treated as a mere means, and therefore wrongly, even if he is also treated as an end in the positive sense. Some of the purposes for whose achievement he is made to serve as a means may be morally objectionable. The fact that one of the ends—the happiness of others—is morally required does not make the action right. Thus, a person could treat another as an end in the positive sense while acting contrary to the duty to treat him as an end in the negative way. This is a consequence of the fact that in treating someone as a means one may be seeking to fulfill several ends, some of which are good and some of which are bad.

These points suggest a serious difficulty. In order to bring this out, I shall again consider certain standard objections to utilitarianism. Several philosophers have contended that utilitarian theory cannot account for the obligations to tell the truth and to keep promises. They have also insisted that such theories cannot accommodate certain dictates of justice. In lying to someone, breaking a promise, or committing an injustice, one could at the same time maximize pleasure or happiness. Thus described, the action would be right according to utilitarianism. (The tendency of some philosophers has been to adjust the theory in such a way that it applies to rules rather than actions. It has then been urged that the rules regarding truth-telling, promise-keeping, and fair-dealing can be supported on utilitarian grounds.)[5] Another objection to utilitarianism can be stated in terms of treating persons as mere means. Someone may treat a person merely as a means in order to procure the greatest possible happiness; in such cases, some people are sacrificed for the sake of the welfare of others. An initial acquaintance with Kant's principle would lead almost everyone to believe that, because of his emphasis on dignity and respect, his moral theory is vastly superior to utilitarian accounts. Perhaps the most surprising ramification of the present inquiry, however, is that in one very significant respect Kant's theory has the same defect as the principle of utility.

5. Several of the most important recent articles on this subject are contained in *Contemporary Utilitarianism*, ed. Michael D. Bayles (Garden City, N.Y.: Doubleday, 1968). Thorough critical discussions of a variety of utilitarian positions are provided by David Lyons in *Forms and Limits of Utilitarianism* (London: Oxford University Press, 1965).

Kant's criterion for treating a person merely as a means is to treat someone as a means to an end which he cannot rationally share as a moral agent possessing autonomy. If all of the ends for which a person is used as a means are morally acceptable, he is treated as an end and the action is not wrong. Suppose, then, that one treats someone as a means to the happiness of others. Suppose further that there is no other end for whose achievement he is used. Can he, on the basis of Kant's view, be treated as a mere means? The answer must be "no." The happiness of others is an obligatory end, and as such, it can be rationally shared by all human beings. Kant uses the concept of men as ends and means in such a way that it is logically impossible for the person in this example to be treated merely as a means.

Kant's theory and utilitarian theory are in this respect in the same ethical boat. He has analyzed his injunction against treating people as mere means in such a way that his position is unable to account for this simple objection based on our ordinary moral beliefs. A utilitarian who tried to avoid the objection by insisting that he would never regard an action involving the treatment of someone as a means to happiness to be a treatment of someone as a mere means would not be taken seriously; he could also say that any untruth leading to the greatest happiness is not to be considered a lie. The inadequacies of the utilitarian position would not in this way be eliminated or even diminished. Despite its apparent superiority, Kant's theory is inadequate for the same reasons.

7   HUMAN DIGNITY

Kant's principle of personality appears to be related to the concept of human dignity. His emphasis on the absolute value of human beings is an important feature of his ethical theory. This notion of value is a difficult one, and it is not clear exactly why he attributes this quality to persons. Yet it is of interest to focus closely on what he says about the matter, for it is in just this respect that his theory is superior to utilitarianism. As has been argued thus far, Kant's analysis of the second formula in terms of "sharing ends" diminishes its appeal. The force of previous criticisms may be minimized by a concentration on his claims about the dignity of human beings.

MORAL WORTH AND HUMAN VALUE

Kant holds that human beings have a value which is absolute, or unconditioned. He does not claim that persons are the only things of value—many things, he believes, are good or valuable—but the value which human beings have is distinctive. As has been shown in Chapter 1, the peculiar character of their worth is linked to their status as ends-in-themselves. Furthermore, his value makes of man himself the object for the moral law and provides the essential foundation for a categorical imperative. The notion of dignity is often utilized in order to characterize this worth. Consider the following famous passage:

> In the kingdom of ends everything has either a *price* or a *dignity*. If it has a price, something else can be put in its place as an *equivalent;* if it is exalted above all price and so admits of no equivalent, then it has a dignity.
> What is relative to universal human inclinations and needs has a *market price;* what, even without presupposing a need, accords with

a certain taste—that is, with satisfaction in the mere purposeless play of our mental powers—has a *fancy price* (*Affektionspreis*); but that which constitutes the sole condition under which anything can be an end in itself has not merely a relative value—that is, a price—but has an intrinsic value—that is, *dignity*. (*GW* 102)

Kant must hold that persons have intrinsic value in order to support the claim that all persons are ends-in-themselves who ought not to be treated merely as means. It is clear, however, from what immediately follows this passage in the *Groundwork*, that he is primarily interested in providing an understanding of moral worth, or virtue, as having dignity. One function of these remarks is thus to amplify and reinforce his earlier claims about the good will, which he says is the only thing conceivable "in the world, or even out of it, which can be taken as good without qualification" (*GW* 61).

Understood in relation to the good will, Kant's statements about dignity may perhaps be construed as claims about persons who have a particular moral character. But Kant quite clearly believes that *all* persons have the status of ends-in-themselves. And this status is dependent upon their having a value which is not merely relative. If being an end-in-itself is dependent upon the possession of absolute value and if all persons are ends-in-themselves, then each person must have dignity or absolute value. But if absolute value depends on virtue or the good will, then not all persons have it. And if this is so, not all persons are ends-in-themselves. Our task in following the principle of personality, however, is to treat all persons, not merely the good or virtuous ones, as ends; we are not allowed to treat even bad people as mere means. These points suggest several important questions. What things, in Kant's view, have dignity? Do persons have a value which is independent of whatever virtue they may have achieved? If they do, what is this value based upon and which of man's characteristics give him this quality?

In the passage quoted above, Kant identifies dignity with intrinsic value. This sort of value may be characterized as follows: *a thing has intrinsic value if its value is not limited to its usefulness as a means, if it has value in itself*. This notion appears to be related to the second formula of the categorical imperative. But

Kant also has another characterization of dignity (*Würde*). In a somewhat later section he makes the following claim: "For nothing can have a value other than that determined for it by the law. But the law-making which determines all value must for this reason have a dignity—that is, an unconditioned and incomparable worth—for the appreciation of which, as necessarily given by a rational being, the word *'reverence'* is the only becoming expression. *Autonomy* is therefore the ground of the dignity of human nature and of every rational nature" (*GW* 103). The identification of dignity, in this passage, with an "unconditioned and incomparable worth" suggests that intrinsic value is not sufficient for dignity. Kant's remarks about dignity betray a certain amount of terminological confusion. There is a difference between intrinsic value and absolute value. It is impossible to reconcile all apparent inconsistencies with regard to this matter, and Kant himself does not attend carefully to this distinction. It is nonetheless very important.

Examples illustrating the two kinds of value may serve to make the distinction clear. Kant appears to hold that both happiness and natural perfection have intrinsic value. We have an obligation to seek our own natural perfection as a value in itself, and not merely as a means to the achievement of other ends. Happiness also has a value which is not limited to its usefulness, either for self-interested ends or for character development. Happiness and natural perfection, however, are not unconditionally valuable. Their goodness is qualified by the virtue (and thus the state of the will) of persons. The good will is, by contrast, absolutely valuable.

The following passage indicates the different kinds of value possessed by virtue and happiness:

> Power, wealth, honour, even health and that complete well-being and contentment with one's state which goes by the name of *'happiness'*, produces boldness, and as a consequence often over-boldness as well, unless a good will is present by which their influence on the mind—and so too the whole principle of action—may be corrected and adjusted to universal ends; not to mention that a rational and impartial spectator can never feel approval in contemplating the uninterrupted prosperity of a being graced by no touch of a pure and

good will, and that consequently a good will seems to constitute the indispensable condition of our very worthiness to be happy. (*GW* 61)

Kant believes that happiness possesses only a conditioned value, while the worth of the good will or moral perfection is absolute. A distinction of this sort is essential in order to render plausible Kant's view that although the highest good (as a union of virtue and happiness) has intrinsic value, happiness is to be apportioned in accordance with virtue (*CPR* 114–15). Since virtue is the condition of man's worthiness to be happy, justice requires that a person be happy only to the extent that he is good. It is in just this respect that the value possessed by virtue is superior to that possessed by happiness. It would therefore seem proper to reserve the term 'dignity' for the former.

Here, however, we encounter a difficult problem. Kant holds that human beings themselves, regardless, apparently, of whatever moral character they may have attained, have dignity or absolute value. He says:

Persons, therefore, are not merely subjective ends whose existence as an object of our actions has a value *for us*: they are *objective ends*—that is, things whose existence is in itself an end, and indeed an end such that in its place we can put no other end to which they should serve *simply* as means; for unless this is so, nothing at all of *absolute* value would be found anywhere. But if all value were conditioned—that is, contingent—then no supreme principle could be found for reason at all. (*GW* 96)

In this and other passages Kant tends to insist on the absolute value of one thing while denying it to everything else. Yet if his main claims about the good will, the highest good, and the principle of personality are to be coherent, *both* the good will and human beings must have dignity. In one sense, human beings have equal value, while in another sense they do not. Insofar as a creature is a human being (and thus is a rational agent) he possesses dignity and is irreplaceable. In this respect no individual has a worth greater than that possessed by anyone else. It is because of this kind of absolute value that one ought to treat persons as ends-in-themselves and never as mere means. Human beings do not obtain this worth; it is not something one can develop or achieve. By contrast, persons who are virtuous have an additional absolute value which also has no price. This sort of value is relevant to what one should receive—how happy he deserves to be—in the determination of the highest good. But it is not relevant to the claim that persons are ends-in-themselves.

Some of Kant's remarks are confusing and misleading with regard to this matter: "Now morality is the only condition under which a rational being can be an end in himself; for only through this is it possible to be a law-making member in a kingdom of ends. Therefore morality, and humanity so far as it is capable of morality, is the only thing which has dignity. Skill and diligence in work have a market price; wit, lively imagination, and humour have a fancy price; but fidelity to promises and kindness based on principle (not on instinct) have an intrinsic worth" (*GW* 102). The use of the term 'morality' is worthy of examination. I have noted that all persons—not just the morally good ones—are ends-in-themselves. This passage initially appears to conflict with this claim but can be utilized in its support. Morality as the good will (or virtue) is not here being claimed to be the end-in-itself. Such an interpretation would be in error for two reasons. In the first place, morality is the *condition* under which something can be an end-in-itself. It is not identified with the end-in-itself. Secondly, 'morality' in this context must refer, not to virtue or an achieved good will, but to the moral law which is "within" each man because of his autonomy. This may be established through attention to Kant's remark that "only through this [only through morality] is it possible to be a law-making member in a kingdom of ends." It is clear that in Kant's view all persons are law-making agents. High moral character is not essential to this status. A person is a moral agent with an autonomous will by virtue of his law-making capacity—his power of self-legislation. Kant says that rational agents are subject to laws arising from their own self-legislating wills: they are required to obey only those rules of which they themselves are sources. This is something which is essential to their freedom and without which they could not be rightly regarded as morally responsible beings.

These considerations concerning dignity and autonomy are substantiated by Kant's claim that "law-making" itself has dignity or unconditioned worth (*GW* 103). In the passage quoted in the preceding paragraph, this point is obscured by Kant's insistence that morally worthy actions have dignity. In the *Groundwork* Kant alternates between emphasis on the dignity of virtue and emphasis on the dignity of human beings. These shifts are to some extent quite understandable. For though the dignity of human beings as ends-in-themselves is not dependent upon the attainment of moral worth or the development of a good will, it is by no means entirely unrelated to the concept of morality. Kant says that humanity has dignity "so far as it is capable of morality." Presumably what he means is that each human being—so far as *he* is capable of morality—possesses dignity. In order to have absolute worth, then, a being must be capable of acting in accordance with the moral law and capable of doing so because of duty. But it is just this capacity which is necessarily linked to man's autonomy as a self-legislating "creator" of the moral law. Indeed, the self-legislative faculty is a necessary condition for morality. Without this, one's behavior might be in harmony with the moral law, as self-legislated by agents who can attain morality, but it could not be subject to moral appraisal. This is true despite the fact that after speaking of man's capacity for morality as that which gives him dignity, Kant gives examples of specific actions which have dignity because of an attained moral worth—an instance of the shift to which I have alluded.

Even more striking examples of Kant's alternating emphasis on the dignity of virtue and the dignity of human beings occur in the following passage:

From what was said a little time ago we can now easily explain how it comes about that, although in the concept of duty we think of subjection to the law, yet we also at the same time attribute to the person who fulfils all his duties a certain sublimity and *dignity*. For it is not in so far as he is *subject* to the law that he has sublimity, but rather in so far as, in regard to this very same law, he is at the same time its *author* and is subordinated to it only on this ground. We have also shown above how neither fear nor inclination, but solely reverence for the law, is the motive which can give an action moral worth. Our own will, provided it were to act only under the condition of being able to make universal law by means of its maxims—this ideal will which can be ours is the proper object of reverence; and the dignity of man consists precisely in his capacity to make universal law, although only on condition of being himself also subject to the law he makes. (*GW* 107)

Some of the difficulties in these remarks can be explained or eliminated with the use of a distinction elucidated in Chapter 3. Kant has two conceptions of the will, though he himself does not always distinguish between them. The Wille, or the self-legislating will, is present in each man as an autonomous rational agent. It is because he possesses this will that man is the source of the moral law. This concept of the will is essentially related to the concept of sharing ends. The other conception of the will is identified with a different aspect of morality. In particular situations a person may decide, as a free agent, to act either in accordance with the moral law or in violation of it. His freedom to perform these actions involves an exercise of his Willkür, his active or deciding will. The attainment of moral worth or virtue is dependent upon this kind of willing. One's Willkür may be either good or bad. In his statement that a good will is the only thing having an unconditioned and incomparable worth, Kant must be understood as speaking of a good Willkür, despite his use of the term *Wille* in that context (*GW* 61).[1] Two basic reasons support this claim. First, the Wille is in a sense always "good": its very nature as the source of the moral law insures that all rules derived from it (those which it legislates) will be perfectly rational and morally acceptable. Since it could not be "bad," it is not this will which one develops in striving to be virtuous or performing a morally worthy action. Secondly, everyone who is a rational agent possesses a Wille, or self-legislating will. It is obvious, however, that not everyone has a good will. If everyone had a good will, everyone would be virtuous. But although everyone has a capacity for virtuous action, human beings vary notoriously in moral character.

The distinction between Wille and Willkür is useful in sorting

1. As Beck has pointed out, Kant is not always consistent in his use of the terms *Wille* and *Willkür*. See Beck, *Kant's Critique of Practical Reason*, pp. 176–77.

out Kant's somewhat confusing claims about dignity. I shall begin with the general claim that whatever dignity anyone possesses is essentially related to some feature of his will. The dignity to be attributed to him is dependent, in one respect, upon the moral worth of his actions. A virtuous person has dignity because he has a good will, a good Willkür. It is this sort of dignity which is possessed by "the person who fulfils all his duties" (*GW* 107), by the person who practices "fidelity to promises and kindness based on principle" (*GW* 102). And it is for this reason that Kant says that "this ideal will which can be ours is the proper object of reverence" (*GW* 107). In this sense not everyone possesses dignity or absolute worth. In another sense, however, all human beings have this quality; for everyone has a Wille, or self-legislative will, by virtue of which he is the source of the moral law. Kant says that one's sublimity is due to his being the "author" of the law and that "the dignity of man consists precisely in his capacity to make universal law" (*GW* 107).

It is in this respect that each man is an end-in-himself. Only this kind of interpretation can render coherent the following views in the texts: (1) all persons are ends-in-themselves who ought not to be treated merely as means; (2) man's status as an end is essentially connected with his dignity or absolute worth; (3) man's autonomy is the ground of his dignity as a rational agent; and (4) virtue or the good will possesses an unconditioned or absolute value.

Without the distinction between Wille and Willkür we would have to deny one of these. Lewis White Beck makes use of the distinction to solve a problem in Kantian studies concerning the concept of freedom. In one sense, only persons who act morally can be free. The difficulty with this is that one could not rightly be held responsible for his decisions to perform morally wrong actions. The Wille/Willkür distinction allows for two concepts of freedom and will, on the basis of which this problem can be resolved. One can be free (and thus morally responsible) even though he does not do what is right (and thus does not follow the dictates of his Wille).[2]

2. Ibid., pp. 176–81.

Although we need not delve into Beck's discussion of this problem, his account is worth noting, for I have attempted to utilize the concepts of Wille and Willkür in a similar manner. Just as, in one sense, only moral persons (and morally acceptable actions) are free, it is also true that in one sense only virtuous persons (and morally worthy actions) have dignity. And just as one cannot be held responsible unless he is free, he may be treated merely as a means unless he has dignity. The reason for this is that one's status as an end-in-oneself is dependent upon the possession of a value which is absolute. Indeed, the possession of such value is what is involved in a person's being an "objective end" (*GW* 96). There must then be another sense in which persons have dignity, just as there is another sense in which they are free.

DIGNITY AND PRICE

In this section, I shall try to provide a better understanding of Kant's views about human beings as possessors of dignity. Kant contrasts that which has dignity with that which has a price. This distinction is made in terms of the ideas of equivalence and replaceability. Kant is primarily concerned with elucidating the notion of dignity as it applies to actions and to motives (as well as to what he calls "attitudes of mind"). He says that skill and diligence have a market price, that wit and imagination have a fancy price, but that promise-keeping has an intrinsic worth (*GW* 102). (In accordance with the points made in the earlier part of the discussion, I shall assume that Kant is attributing absolute or unconditioned value, rather than mere intrinsic value, to virtuous actions.) As I have noted, however, there is a sense in which all men, regardless of their moral character and of the moral quality of their actions, have dignity. Presumably the notions of equivalence and replaceability must be utilized in a sound account of man's value as well as in an account of the dignity of virtue. For if human beings can be replaced and admit of equivalents, then they have only a price, not dignity. And if they do not have dignity or absolute value, they are not ends-in-themselves. But in just what respects does Kant believe persons to be irreplaceable?

Kant does not supply examples to show how the notion of value applies to persons as well as to actions and qualities. He does, however, appear to believe that human beings cannot be replaced by anything else. Consider a passage quoted previously: "Persons, therefore, are not merely subjective ends whose existence as an object of our actions has a value *for us:* they are *objective ends*—that is, things whose existence is in itself an end, and indeed an end such that in its place we can put no other end to which they should serve *simply* as means; for unless this is so, nothing at all of *absolute* value would be found anywhere" (*GW* 96). According to this, there is at least one sort of equivalent of which persons do not admit: nothing can be put in the place of a person for the sake of which that individual should serve merely as a means.

Kant here speaks of persons in much the same way that he later speaks of virtuous actions. He says of good actions that nothing can be put in their place. Although he does not claim that they should not be used merely as means, he does say that their worth does not consist "in the effects which result from them" or "in the advantage or profit they produce" (*GW* 102). He holds, then, though he does not say this explicitly, that their value is not limited to their usefulness as means. They have an intrinsic worth. The use of the German word *innern* (translated by Paton as 'intrinsic') is significant.[3] The value of the good will and of those morally worthy actions in which such a will is manifested is "internal." The goodness of an action is not dependent upon its consequences. If it were, then any action having those consequences would presumably be good. The action would be replaceable and would thus admit of some equivalent.

It is important to note that Kant is not saying that such actions ought never to serve as means. Neither is he denying that they have a value which *is* dependent upon their consequences. It is possible to view fidelity with respect to promises as a means to other ends, for example, one's own self-interest; it is possible, that is, to form a hypothetical imperative of some such form as "If you do not wish to be punished, you had better keep all your

3. The reader may wish to consult the Academy edition, vol. 4, p. 435.

promises." This sort of judgment within a particular sphere—that of prudence or self-interest—is perfectly legitimate. Kant would hold, however, that one must go beyond such imperatives and understand that there is a categorical imperative commanding promise-keeping quite apart from its personal advantages. In order for there to be such an imperative, promise-keeping must have more than a mere market price or use. It must have dignity.

Similar points may be made about the claim that human beings have value. We have seen that Kant holds that human beings are irreplaceable and admit of no equivalents. One might object to this on the ground that there are some respects in which human beings can be replaced. But even if this is so, it may still be insisted that they have dignity. Baseball players, for example, can sometimes be replaced. If some particular player is injured, another player may come off the bench to take his place. The second player might even be just as good as the first. In this way one can be substituted for another, and each player may admit of an equivalent. Are we to conclude, then, that baseball players have a market price? If the situation I have described is conceivable (and it clearly is, for such substitutions occur very frequently in baseball games), then we cannot deny that they do have such a price.

What should be noticed here is that the respects in which the players can be replaced are just those respects in which they are *useful*. This, of course, is one sense in which people, qualities, and things are valuable. When a baseball player receives the Most Valuable Player award, he is not being honored for his dignity or intrinsic worth. His value is, rather, a worth to his team. Kant holds, however, that persons have a value which does not depend upon their being valuable to other people or for the pursuit of goals. It might be claimed that some particularly outstanding player is irreplaceable and so valuable that no substitute is adequate. Here as well, the notion of dignity need not be involved. For the claim might be understood simply as a contention that no other player happens to be as useful, that no other player can in fact do the job as well. In principle, however, there could be such a player who is just as useful. If he were available, then the other player would be replaceable. The claim that one or the other is indispensible is dependent for its verification upon some assessment of available baseball talent. Its validity is also dependent upon the circumstances which happen to obtain. To hold that a person has dignity, however, involves the claim that under no circumstances whatever can persons be replaced: dignity, unlike market price, does not depend upon usefulness. Kant's claim is suggestive of certain commonsense beliefs about how persons ought to be treated. There is often the complaint in baseball and other sports that players are simply bought and sold as are other goods in the marketplace. There is the idea that to treat them in this way is to treat them merely as baseball players rather than also as persons. To use Kant's language, it is to treat them merely as having a market price rather than also as having dignity.

This notion of value is helpful in providing another way of understanding the principle of personality. To treat a person merely as a means may be viewed as a way of treating him merely as having instrumental value. The difference between treating a person as an end and treating him as a means is analogous to the contrast between treating him as having intrinsic value and treating him as having instrumental value. To treat a person as an end-in-himself may be understood as treating him as having intrinsic value. One need not be bothered here by the fact that the term 'end' is most often used in the sense of 'goal' or 'purpose'. The emphasis is upon *treating persons as ends,* and this need not suggest the treatment of them as goals or aims. Treating a person as an end may be understood as treating him in some of the ways in which one treats his ends. The most important of these ways is this: one treats his ends as having value. And the way one treats a human being as an end-in-himself having absolute value may be understood as analogous to the way one treats his most important ends, for the sake of which all else is subordinated. Kant does not formulate the principle in this way. But it is certainly within the spirit of his moral philosophy.

The plausibility of this way of understanding the principle may be shown by further attention to the distinction between hypothetical and categorical imperatives. Kant holds that in order for actions such as fidelity to promises to be commanded categorically, they must have an intrinsic value. For if their value is limited to their usefulness, then they ought to be performed only if the agent possesses an end for which they can be used as means. This can yield only a hypothetical imperative. Kant appears to believe that categorical imperatives can exist only if there also exist actions having intrinsic value. He also appears to believe that in order for there to be categorical imperatives, persons must have a value which is absolute. If they have merely instrumental value, then certain actions affecting their well-being or existence could be commanded only hypothetically.

Kant contrasts the value which persons possess with the value that ends (in the ordinary sense of "adopted purposes") have:

> Ends that a rational being adopts arbitrarily as *effects* of his action (material ends) are in every case only relative; for it is solely their relation to special characteristics in the subject's power of appetition which gives them their value. Hence this value can provide no universal principles, no principles valid and necessary for all rational beings and also for every volition—that is, no practical laws. Consequently all these relative ends can be the ground only of hypothetical imperatives.

> Suppose, however, there were something *whose existence* has *in itself* an absolute value, something which as *an end in itself* could be a ground of determinate laws; then in it, and in it alone, would there be the ground of a possible categorical imperative—that is, of a practical law. (*GW* 95)

He then goes on to insist that persons are ends-in-themselves with absolute value. He appears to believe that one cannot consistently hold that there must be categorical rather than hypothetical imperatives and at the same time deny that human beings have absolute worth.

Thus far I have characterized treating something as having only a market price as treating it exclusively in terms of its uses. If the owners of baseball teams treat their players only in terms of their usefulness—and consequently buy and sell them as they might buy and sell used cars—they treat them as having market values. To treat a person as having only a market price is to treat him as having value only *to* or *for* some other person or some particular goal. How does market price differ from fancy price? Kant says that those things which have a fancy price accord with some particular taste. He characterizes taste as "satisfaction in the mere purposeless play of our mental powers" (*GW* 102). He indicates further that, unlike market price, fancy price does not presuppose a particular need or goal. He offers humor and imagination as examples of things which possess this kind of value. What Kant appears to be suggesting with the contrast between fancy and market price is similar to Hume's distinction between qualities which are "immediately agreeable" and those which are "useful."[4] Despite the difference between these two sorts of value, however, there is one immensely important respect in which they are alike: each is an instance of a merely *relative* kind of value; they do not have their value solely "in themselves." Whatever value is possessed by that which has only a market price is relative to (and thus dependent upon) some purpose or aim for which it can be used. And whatever value is possessed by that which has only a fancy price is relative to someone's valuing, desiring, or liking it. Both values are due to something *external* to the valuable objects themselves.

The absolute worth of human beings is radically different from either of these. Persons have a dignity or unconditioned value wholly independent of being valuable for or valued by anything else. There is an interesting way in which this notion relates to some ordinary beliefs about persons whom we consider to have dignity. We sometimes think of individuals as having dignity in proportion to their independence. One may have a feeling of self-respect or a sense of dignity because he has been able to become independent, for instance, of his parents or the government. The word 'dignity' frequently occurs in discussions of the welfare system. It has often been alleged that a person caught within the system and dependent upon government assistance is unable to live with the dignity possessed by those who can do without it. Here we find the suggestion that dignity is importantly connected with being able to "stand on one's own feet" and to be, at least in this admittedly limited financial sense, independent. Another context for this popular connection between dignity and inde-

4. See David Hume, *An Enquiry Concerning the Principles of Morals* (1777), chaps. 6–8.

pendence is in discussion of the lives of certain politicians. It is often said of some vice-presidents that they do not have dignity because of their excessive dependence upon the wishes and fortunes of others (especially, of course, the presidents whom they serve and by whom their loyalty is demanded). This is frequently expressed in the criticism that "he is not his own man."

This ordinary notion of dignity is not specifically what Kant has in mind in saying that human beings have absolute value. One obvious difference is that, as the term is used in these examples, not everyone has dignity; while in Kant's view all persons do have absolute worth. Another difference is that there may be, in this ordinary sense, degrees of dignity in proportion to the extent of the independence one possesses, while in Kant's view, men have equal value. The important point, nevertheless, is that there appears to be a significant connection between dignity and independence. Persons have dignity because they are not dependent for their value upon the purposes or preferences of anyone else.

The idea of independence is useful in demonstrating the plausibility of Kant's claim that autonomy is "the ground of the dignity of human nature and of every rational nature" (*GW* 103). To be free of something is to have a kind of independence with regard to it. There is an important sense in which the welfare recipients and the vice-presidents are not free, since many of their actions—indeed an important segment of their lives—are conditioned by the actions and desires of others and there is much that they are not free to do. There appears to be, via the notion of independence, a connection between freedom and dignity. (It should not be surprising that slavery—clearly a paradigm case of depriving persons of the freedom we believe they ought to have—is a case of treating human beings merely as means. This is a foremost reason why so many have alleged that keeping a person as a slave is a way of acting contrary to his dignity. In the United States slaves were once treated as having, quite literally, only a "market price.")

This idea may be plausibly applied to Kant's view of human beings as free of causal chains in the phenomenal realm. He believes that in order for there to be moral actions man must be free of the causal necessity to which material objects are subject. Human action, as opposed to mere behavior, is thus "internal" in the sense that it is not dependent upon some prior cause (*CPR* 89–90). Man, as understood from the "noumenal" point of view, is independent of nature.[5] As we have seen already, Kant believes that autonomy is a necessary condition for freedom. Man's possession of autonomy involves his being bound only by laws which he himself has willed. All of man's moral obligations are thus based on his own self-legislative capacity as a possessor of Wille. In this way human beings are not dependent upon anything external which they ought to obey. All laws which God or the government might lay down must conform to what persons themselves as rational beings can will. A person's willing is valuable quite apart from whether or not it accords with what someone else might approve or command.[6]

Kant appears to believe that this sort of independence is essential to morality. If what he says about this matter is plausible, then the absolute value of human beings is necessary for the existence of morality. Similarly, Kant holds that man's capacity for morality is that which gives him dignity and makes him an end-in-himself (*GW* 102). But man's capacity for morality is necessary in order for him to be a responsible moral agent. If it is true of anyone that he *ought* to do something, it is necessary that he be a moral agent. If Kant is right and if my amplification of the relevant textual passages is accurate, then the absolute worth of human beings cannot be denied if one at the same time wishes to insist that human beings are moral agents who have obligations.

This claim can be supported further by reference to the distinction between categorical and hypothetical imperatives.[7] Human beings can have a fancy price as well as dignity. A person

5. Cf. Beck, *Kant's Critique of Practical Reason*, p. 103.

6. Some of Kant's remarks in Part I of *The Metaphysics of Morals*, in which he sometimes says that one has an absolute obligation to obey the law, appear to conflict with these points. See, for example, Immanuel Kant, *The Metaphysical Elements of Justice* [Part I of *The Metaphysics of Morals*], trans. John Ladd (Indianapolis: Bobbs-Merrill, 1965), pp. 84–85.

7. A thorough account of Kant's views on imperatives may be found in Lewis White Beck, "Apodictic Imperatives," in *Studies in the Philosophy of Kant* (Indianapolis: Bobbs-Merrill, 1965), pp 177–99.

might be valued, for example, solely because he is humorous and enjoyable to be with; he might, that is, simply accord with the "tastes" of others. Kant says that the value of ends adopted as the effects of an action is relative because "it is solely their relation to special characteristics in the subject's power of appetition which gives them their value" (*GW* 95). Persons themselves may also have such a value. In this regard they would have a value which is neither limited to their usefulness nor due to their status as ends-in-themselves. The value would still, however, be only relative. The person would be valuable because of his relation to the desires of others. But it does not follow from this that he would not have dignity. And if someone treated him as having only a fancy price—as being valuable only because he is valued by others—he would not be treating him as an end-in-himself.

VALUES AND CATEGORICAL IMPERATIVES

There are important relationships between dignity and categorical imperatives and between price and hypothetical imperatives. An account of these connections may serve to demonstrate why Kant's principle of personality is attractive. Consider the following simple imperative: "Do not kill others." Kant considered this to be a particular categorical imperative derivable from the general formula for all such imperatives. It may be understood as categorical despite the fact that there may be exceptions to it in very special circumstances. If it is categorical, the action (or in this case the omission of an action—refraining from killing) is commanded unconditionally. This means that it is not viewed merely as a means to the satisfaction of some desire. Could such an imperative be sound if human beings have only fancy prices and market prices, that is, value merely *to* certain people and *for* the attainment of purposes?

It would be quite possible to establish hypothetical imperatives on the assumption that persons do not have dignity but have a relative value. Suppose that some man, A, is of value to another person, B. A and B are in business together. If either A or B dies, then the other stands to lose a large amount of money. Because of the way in which their respective fortunes are related, B may reasonably view A's continued existence as a means to his own economic welfare. He quite clearly has reason not to kill A and good reasons to keep A from being killed by others. He also has reason to help keep him from contracting incurable diseases and, in general, to do whatever he can to help preserve his existence. These reasons may be expressed in the form of hypothetical imperatives addressed to B, who asks, "Ought I to preserve A's existence?" The answer would be as follows: "Yes, because you have certain ends, X, Y, and Z; and A is a necessary means to those ends. The preservation of A's life is thus a necessary means to the attainment of your ends. In order to be rational you ought not to kill (and otherwise ought to try to preserve) A." It would seem clear that Kant is right in insisting that moral obligations cannot be derived from the principles on which this sort of imperative is based. For in this case what someone ought to do is based solely on considerations relating to that person's self-interest and to his desires and aims. In Kant's view moral imperatives must apply (at least somewhat) independently of the particular desires of the agent. The case under consideration is one in which a person is viewed merely as a means, and the only sort of imperative that can apply is hypothetical.

The other sort of relative value—fancy price—might also yield a hypothetical imperative. Suppose that C and D are very close friends. They have strong feelings of admiration and affection for one another and derive much pleasure from their relationship. C and D do not, however, value each other merely as means: they do not think of each other as being useful only to the achievement of purposes. They value each other "even without presupposing a need," and their valuation is due to what we may call their "tastes." D quite clearly has good reason to help in the preservation of C's life, for if C were to die, D would become most unhappy. In this case there could be a hypothetical imperative based on Kant's general claim that each man wills and seeks his own happiness. Though it is difficult to imagine D's asking for advice about the matter, an imperative might be addressed to him somewhat as follows: "You derive a great deal of happiness from C, and you certainly seek your own happiness. Therefore you ought to preserve C's life." It is not essential that D view C merely as a means in order to show that such an imperative can be only hypothetical. (Even though C's existence may be a means to D's happiness, D does not value C merely as a means). The reasons given with the issuance of the imperative relate solely to D's desires and to what would make him happy. If a person were said to be valuable only in this sense, his value would be merely relative, because (to borrow Kant's phrase) it is the person's relation to "special characteristics in the subject's power of appetition" which gives him value (*GW* 95).

In such cases the interests of the agent are considered to be of paramount importance. The hypothetical imperatives are prudential rather than moral. This point is significantly related to an important feature of the contexts in which the principle of personality is invoked. When a person is condemned for treating another merely as a means, he is often being criticized for what is thought to be selfish behavior. ("He is using another for his own selfish ends.") Selfishness, in virtue of the way the word is most often used, is usually morally wrong. (In this regard it may be contrasted with self-interest.) This is perhaps one reason why the principle is readily accepted by many people as a sound moral guide. Insofar as morality is to be distinguished from mere prudence, it might even plausibly be considered a necessary presupposition of moral judgment and moral reasoning. The denial of such a principle may be tantamount to the denial of morality itself. Such a strong claim, however, is not essential to the present argument.

To treat a person merely as a means is also a way of treating one person as more important than another, of subordinating one individual to the welfare or interests of someone else. As such, it is a violation of the fundamental principles of fair treatment. It is, in other words, a violation of the principle that, barring very special circumstances, persons are to be treated equally. Furthermore, the effort to treat persons as having absolute value would seem to result in a greater likelihood that the moral rules against killing, injuring, and deceiving will actually be followed. This might be called a pragmatic argument for treating persons as ends. Understood in this way, treating persons as ends-in-themselves is valuable as a means to the fulfillment of other moral obligations (though the persons themselves are not viewed as mere means to this end).

If persons had value only in one of these relative ways, there would be no categorical imperatives, no universal principles, "no principles valid and necessary for all rational beings and also for every volition" (GW 95). Many of these points could be extended to other basic categorical imperatives, such as "Do not injure others" and "Do not lie." Actions in accord with these imperatives might often be performed solely because doing so is a means to the agent's ends. If this were the case, the proposition that persons have absolute value would then also be essential to the establishment of these imperatives as categorical ones.[8]

Can we conclude from this discussion that human beings have dignity? Part of the basis for such a conclusion would be that the imperative "Do not kill others" is categorical. One might, of course, deny this claim. I do not see, however, how one can consistently claim a moral (as opposed to a merely prudential) obligation not to do this and at the same time insist that the imperative must be hypothetical. Kant's philosophy specifies that morality must consist in categorical imperatives. Indeed, he believes that unless there are some such imperatives, morality is merely a chimera. One might have a different reason, however, for denying that people have absolute value. He could insist that the imperative "Persons ought not to be killed" does not depend upon human beings' having value. It is difficult to see just how such a claim could be defended. Our commonsense judgments about what things ought and ought not to exist appear to be related to judgments as to whether those things have or do not have value; for example, the reasons given for preserving the redwoods, universities, baseball, or great paintings are given in terms of their value. It is not clear what someone would mean if he were to insist that

---

8. The claim that "Do not lie" is a categorical imperative of the Kantian sort might be thought to conflict with an earlier point (see chapter 5, note 2, above) that Kant is probably wrong in his insistence that lying is always wrong. The two claims, however, are perfectly consistent. It is not necessary that an imperative be exceptionless in order to be categorical. This has been demonstrated by Paton in "An Alleged Right to Lie," pp. 190–203, and by Singer in Generalization in Ethics, pp. 217–33.

something ought to be preserved even though it has no value whatsoever. We make certain definite connections between the value of something and its "right" to exist. Indeed, if something has value, it may have a prima facie claim to exist or to be preserved.

If one is not content to rest his belief that human beings ought not to be destroyed solely on their "market" value or their "fancy" value, it appears that he must conclude that human beings have dignity. It is at least doubtful that, without this value, there could be a categorical imperative involving a moral obligation not to kill persons. This interpretation of the principle of personality provides a way of avoiding a criticism discussed in Chapter 4. The attitudes and motives of the agent are relevant to whether he acts on the basis of either a categorical or a hypothetical imperative. If he acts solely out of self-interest, he may perform many of the actions required by categorical imperatives but he will be *obeying* only hypothetical ones. Furthermore, motives and attitudes are relevant to whether he treats another as having absolute value or merely relative value. They thus become important for determining whether he treats someone as an end-in-himself or merely as a means.[9]

There is still another way in which someone might wish to deny that human beings have absolute value. He might insist that B has an obligation not to kill A, not because A's continued existence has value for B, but because his preservation is in the interests of *other* persons. The imperative would then not be merely prudential, because the desires and interests of people other than the agent are brought into consideration. A utilitarian, for instance, might insist that the end which persons ought to seek is happiness or pleasure. Whatever action is conducive to the maximization of happiness will, according to such a theory, be considered obligatory.

An example may make this clear. The utilitarian theorist might point out that B ought not to kill A because A's death would

9. One of Kant's claims about punishment indicates just how motives and attitudes may be relevant. He says that if one punishes a criminal because doing so will be of advantage to society, one treats him merely as a means (Kant, *The Metaphysical Elements of Justice*, p. 100).

cause much suffering and unhappiness for his family. A might be quite useful to his wife and children in providing for their basic needs. Without him they would be forced to alter their lives considerably and to assume the burden of providing these things for themselves at the expense of their self-development. The imperative not to kill A would then be based on the fact that he is a means to the welfare of others. He is thus viewed as having instrumental value, or a market price.

A person who obeys the imperative only for these reasons would be treating the other as having value merely as a means. If some machine had been providing the food, shelter, and clothing for these people, then B would have just as much reason—and just as much of a moral obligation—not to destroy it as not to kill A. But there might be different reasons for the issuance of the imperative. Suppose that A's family derives much pleasure and enjoyment from him and that they value him quite apart from his uses to them. A utilitarian might insist that, for these reasons as well, his death would make others unhappy and ought not to take place. On these grounds, such a theorist could conceivably contend that there is a categorical imperative requiring B to preserve A despite the fact that (as the theorist contends) A has no absolute or intrinsic value.

It is important to see how this admittedly sketchy version of utilitarianism clashes with Kant's ethical theory when the concept of absolute value is emphasized. It is also of interest to view Kant's position apart from his stress on shared ends as a criterion for treating persons as ends-in-themselves. The emphasis on the notion of absolute value makes Kant's ideas accord much better with the initial impression that his theory provides an attractive and humane alternative to utilitarianism. As we saw in Chapter 6, Kant holds that the happiness of others is an objective end which all persons ought to promote. This end is one in which every person can share. But even if one is treated as a means to an end in which he can share, he may be treated at the same time as having only instrumental value—he may not be treated as having dignity. If being treated with dignity is essential to being treated as an end-in-oneself, one would in such a case not be treated in accordance with the second formulation of the **categorical imperative**.

Certain important contrasts between Kant's view and this version of utilitarianism are readily apparent. If the two theories are in these respects radically different, which is superior? I shall not attempt to provide a completely defensible answer to this question. I shall, however, indicate why I believe Kant's view to be superior to utilitarianism and to accord much better with our deepest intuitions about morality. The utilitarian reasons for not killing A cannot provide a categorical imperative of the Kantian sort, for the action is viewed merely as a means to some end, not as valuable in itself. This is one basic way in which Kant differentiates hypothetical from categorical imperatives: "If the action would be good solely as a means *to something else,* the imperative is *hypothetical;* if the action is represented as good *in itself* and therefore as necessary, in virtue of its principle, for a will which of itself accords with reason, then the imperative is *categorical"* (*GW* 82). This passage does not show, however, that what Kant calls hypothetical imperatives are not moral ones. The utilitarian might reject Kant's account of categorical imperatives as well as his account of the ultimate ends of human action. It is important, nonetheless, to recognize that within Kant's ethical theory, the absolute value of human beings does appear to be essentially tied to the concept of a categorical imperative.

But are we correct in holding (with Kant) that the duty not to kill people cannot be based solely on their relative value in contributing to the happiness of others? I shall try to indicate why I believe this to be right by taking note of certain consequences of the utilitarian account sketched above. The theory goes against some of our most basic moral beliefs about what may be called "the right to life." According to the theory, human beings have no absolute value and the only reason for a moral imperative not to kill them is that other people would be made unhappy. On these grounds the claim is made that since the killing of A would make others unhappy, one ought not to kill him. We may assume that if others have an obligation not to kill A, then A has a right not to be killed by them. (Rights and duties may not always be correlative, but in this case the claim appears to be reasonable.) What this means, however, is that according to the utilitarian account, A's right not to be killed is conditional on other people's desires—that is, upon the fact that his family wants him to stay alive and upon the fact that they would be unhappy were he to die. Presumably, if no one cared whether A lives, then no one would have an obligation not to kill him. In having no value to or for others—in having no relative value—he would have no right to live. This consequence cannot be avoided if one insists that persons have no absolute value and are thus not ends-in-themselves.

The denial that human beings are ends-in-themselves leads to the denial of some of our most basic beliefs about the right to life. For surely we do not believe that one person's right to live is, in the ways indicated, dependent upon other people's desires and needs. This right is something we believe persons to have "in themselves." Furthermore, we believe that there is a sense in which persons are in this respect equal. From the standpoint of the right to life, the fact that one individual, P, makes others happier than does someone else, Q, does not give P any more of a right than Q not to be killed.

An example may make this clearer. Suppose that an eminent scientist dies in a plane crash caused by a bomb explosion. One can easily imagine many people lamenting the loss of something valuable. They might say such things as the following: "Consider what he might have accomplished if only he had lived," or "It will be hard for us to get along without him," or "We will miss his intellect and his knowledge." The sort of value implied in each of these statements is only relative. Some very sophisticated machine which could do many of the things that the scientist did might also have been destroyed in the plane crash. All of these comments could just as reasonably be made about the machine as about the scientist, and in this respect the machine would have had as much value as did the man. The person who set the bomb could be condemned for destroying two things of value. Yet most of us would surely be inclined to insist that there is a huge difference between the loss of a human being and the loss of the machine. We would insist that in the case of the scientist the right to life has been transgressed and that the saboteur is much more to be condemned for killing the person than for destroying the machine. The sort of utilitarian theory which I have been discussing is unable to account for this fundamental difference in moral judgment. Unless we are prepared to give up these judgments as irrational (at the least, certainly a hasty alternative), we must conclude that human beings have a value apart from their usefulness as means.

There is another judgment that the utilitarian theorist cannot account for. Let us suppose that a person of far less ability and fame was also killed in the plane crash. The murderer thus has killed two individuals of far different relative value. Despite this difference there would be a sense in which we would feel that the same judgment involved in our condemnation of the scientist's murder should also be involved in a condemnation of the other person's murder. Two equally important rights are violated. There is a sense, that is, in which these individuals have equal value. Since they differ with respect to relative value, we must conclude that they have dignity or unconditioned value.

Such versions of utilitarianism de-emphasize the importance of human beings. Pleasure is made the ultimate end for all action. The pleasure that such theorists would probably emphasize is that which human beings can experience. But once pleasure or happiness is made the supreme end, there is no reason why the pleasure of human beings should be preferred (or can rationally be preferred) to that of anything else capable of experiencing it. Sidgwick is consistent here in claiming that the pleasure of all sentient beings ought to be included in hedonistic calculations.[10] Pleasure itself, not pleasure for man, becomes the end-in-itself. Human beings are thus subordinated to another end for which they can serve as mere means. Kant's theory, understood in terms of the concept of absolute value, is strongly opposed to all such views. The arguments I have given provide neither a conclusive refutation of utilitarianism nor a complete defense of Kant. Nevertheless, they indicate how much better his view accords with our deepest and most fundamental intuitions about morality. I have attempted to provide a transcendental argument in the spirit of Kant for the claim that human beings have dignity and are ends-in-themselves.

10. Henry Sidgwick, *The Methods of Ethics* (New York: Dover, 1966), p. 414.

BIBLIOGRAPHY

INDEX

SELECTED BIBLIOGRAPHY

This bibliography contains works which I have found to be of value. I have not tried to provide an exhaustive list of works pertaining to the topic. In addition to sources cited in the text I have included books and articles useful to the reader who wishes to pursue the subject in some depth. (For the English translations of Kant's works listed here, I have indicated the pertinent volume in the Royal Prussian Academy edition of Kant's works.)

Acton, H. B. *Kant's Moral Philosophy*. London: Macmillan, 1970.

Atwell, John E. "Are Kant's First Two Moral Principles Equivalent?," *Journal of the History of Philosophy* 7, no. 3 (July 1969): 273–84.

Bayles, Michael D., ed. *Contemporary Utilitarianism*. Garden City, N.Y.: Doubleday, 1968.

Beck, Lewis White. "Apodictic Imperatives." In *Studies in the Philosophy of Kant*, pp. 177–99. Indianapolis: Bobbs-Merrill, 1965.

———. *A Commentary on Kant's Critique of Practical Reason*. Chicago: University of Chicago Press, 1960.

———. "Kant's two Conceptions of the Will in Their Political Context." In *Studies in the Philosophy of Kant*, pp. 215–29. Indianapolis: Bobbs-Merrill, 1965.

Cohen, Morris R. "A Critique of Kant's Philosophy of Law." In *The Heritage of Kant*, ed. George Tapley Whitney and David F. Bowers, pp. 279–302. Princeton: Princeton University Press, 1939.

Dietrichson, Paul. "What Does Kant Mean by 'Acting from Duty'?" In *Kant: A Collection of Critical Essays*, ed. Robert Paul Wolff, pp. 314–30. Garden City, N.Y.: Doubleday, 1967.

Donagan, Alan. "Is There a Credible Form of Utilitarianism?" In *Contemporary Utilitarianism*, ed. Michael D. Bayles, pp. 187–202. Garden City, N.Y: Doubleday, 1968.

Duncan, A. R. C. *Practical Reason and Morality*. London: Nelson, 1957.

155

Ebbinghaus, Julius. "Interpretation and Misinterpretation of the Categorical Imperative." In *Kant: A Collection of Critical Essays*, ed. Robert Paul Wolff, pp. 211–27. Garden City, N.Y.: Doubleday, 1967.

Gotshalk, D. W. "The Central Doctrine of the Kantian Ethics." In *The Heritage of Kant*, ed. George Tapley Whitney and David F. Bowers, pp. 183–96. New York: Russell & Russell, 1962.

Gregor, Mary J. *Laws of Freedom*. New York: Barnes & Noble, 1963.

Grene, Marjorie. "On Some Distinctions Between Men and Brutes," *Ethics* 57, no. 2 (January 1947): 121–27.

Griffin, James. "Consequences," *Proceedings of the Aristotelian Society* 65 (1964–65): 167–82.

Haezrahi, Pepita. "The Concept of Man as an End-in-Himself." In *Kant: A Collection of Critical Essays*, ed. Robert Paul Wolff, pp. 291–313. Garden City, N.Y.: Doubleday, 1967.

Hall, Robert W. "Kant and Ethical Formalism," *Kant-Studien* 52 (1960–61): 433–39.

Harris, Errol E. "Respect for Persons." In *Ethics and Society*, ed. Richard T. De George, pp. 111–32. Garden City, N.Y.: Doubleday, 1966.

Hoernle, R. F. A. "Kant's Concept of the 'Intrinsic Worth' of Every 'Rational Being'," *The Personalist* 24, no. 2 (April 1943): 130–46.

Holmes, Oliver Wendell. "The Common Law." In *The Mind and Faith of Justice Holmes*, ed. Max Lerner. Boston: Little, Brown, 1951.

Hume, David. *An Enquiry Concerning the Principles of Morals*. La Salle, Ill.: Open Court, 1960.

Jones, W. T. *Morality and Freedom in the Philosophy of Immanuel Kant*. London: Oxford University Press, 1940.

———. "Purpose, Nature, and the Moral Law." In *The Heritage of Kant*, ed. George Tapley Whitney and David F. Bowers, pp. 229–42. New York: Russell & Russell, 1962.

Kant, Immanuel. *Critique of Judgement*, trans. J. H. Bernard. New York: Hafner, 1951. [For German text, see vol. 5 of the Academy edition.]

———. *Critique of Practical Reason*, trans. Lewis White Beck. Indianapolis: Bobbs-Merrill, 1956 [For German text, see vol. 5 of the Academy edition.]

———. *Doctrine of Virtue*, Part II of *The Metaphysics of Morals*. Trans. Mary J. Gregor. New York: Harper & Row, 1964. [For

German text, see vol. 6 of the Academy edition.]

—————. *Groundwork of the Metaphysics of Morals,* trans. H. J. Paton. New York: Harper & Row, 1964. [For German text, see vol. 4 of the Academy edition.]

—————. *Lectures on Ethics,* trans. Louis Infield. New York: Harper & Row, 1963.

—————. *The Metaphysical Elements of Justice,* Part I of *The Metaphysics of Morals.* Trans. John Ladd. Indianapolis: Bobbs-Merrill, 1965. [For German text, see vol. 6 of the Academy edition.]

—————. *Religion Within the Limits of Reason Alone,* trans. Theodore M. Greene and Hoyt H. Hudson. New York: Harper & Row, 1960.

Kemp, John. *The Philosophy of Kant.* London: Oxford University Press, 1968.

Körner, Stephan. *Kant.* Baltimore: Penguin, 1955.

Liddell, Brendan E. A. *Kant on the Foundation of Morality.* Bloomington: Indiana University Press, 1970.

Lindsay, A. D. *Kant.* London: Benn, 1934.

Lyons, David. *Forms and Limits of Utilitarianism.* London: Oxford University Press, 1965.

Maclagan, W. G. "Respect for Persons as a Moral Principle—I," *Philosophy* 35, no. 134 (July 1960): 193–217.

—————. "Respect for Persons as a Moral Principle—II," *Philosophy* 35, no. 135 (October 1960): 289–305.

Mill, John Stuart. *Utilitarianism.* Indianapolis: Bobbs-Merrill, 1957.

Morris, Bertram. "The Dignity of Man," *Ethics* 57, no. 1 (October 1946): 57–64.

Murphy, Arthur E. *The Theory of Practical Reason.* LaSalle, Ill.: Open Court, 1965.

—————. *The Uses of Reason.* New York: Macmillan, 1943.

Murphy, Jeffrie G. *Kant: The Philosophy of Right.* London: Macmillan, 1970.

Nahm, Milton C. " 'Sublimity' and the 'Moral Law' in Kant's Philosophy," *Kant-Studien* 48 (1956–57): 502–24.

Nelson, Leonard. *System of Ethics,* trans. Norbert Guterman. New Haven: Yale University Press, 1956.

Nowell-Smith, Patrick. "Utilitarianism and Treating Others as Ends," *Nous* 1, no. 1 (March 1967): 81–90.

Paton, H. J. "The Aim and Structure of Kant's *Grundlegung,*" *Philosophical Quarterly* 8 (April 1958): 112–30.

—————. "An Alleged Right to Lie: A Problem in Kantian Ethics,"

Kant-Studien 45 (1953–54): 190–203.

——. *The Categorical Imperative.* London: Hutchinson, 1967.

Paulsen, Friedrich. *Immanuel Kant: His Life and Doctrine.* New York: Ungar, 1963.

Reich, Klaus. "Kant and Greek Ethics (II)," *Mind* 48 (1939): 446–63.

Ross, Sir William David. *Kant's Ethical Theory.* Oxford: Oxford University Press, 1954.

Scott-Taggart, M. J. "Recent Work on the Philosophy of Kant," *American Philosophical Quarterly* 3, no. 3 (July 1966): 171–209.

Sidgwick, Henry. *The Methods of Ethics.* New York: Dover, 1966.

——. *Outlines of the History of Ethics.* Boston: Beacon Press, 1960.

Silber, John R. "The Ethical Significance of Kant's *Religion.*" Introduction to Immanuel Kant, *Religion within the Limits of Reason Alone,* trans. Theodore M. Greene and Hoyt H. Hudson, pp. lxxix–cxxxiv. New York: Harper & Row, 1960.

——. "The Importance of the Highest Good in Kant's Ethics," *Ethics* 73, no. 3 (April 1963): 179–97.

——. "Kant's Conception of the Highest Good as Immanent and Transcendent," *Philosophical Review* 68 (1959): 469–92.

——. "The Metaphysical Importance of the Highest Good as the Canon of Pure Reason in Kant's Philosophy," *Texas Studies in Literature and Language* 1 (1959): 233–44.

Singer, Marcus George. *Generalization in Ethics.* New York: Knopf, 1961.

Teale, A. E. *Kantian Ethics.* London: Oxford University Press, 1951.

Wick, Warner. "Introduction" to Immanuel Kant, *The Metaphysical Principles of Virtue,* Part II of *The Metaphysics of Morals.* Trans. James Ellington. Indianapolis: Bobbs-Merrill, 1964.

Williams, T. C. *The Concept of the Categorical Imperative.* Oxford: Oxford University Press, 1968.

Wolff, Robert Paul, ed. Immanuel Kant, *Foundations of the Metaphysics of Morals,* trans. Lewis W. Beck. Indianapolis: Bobbs-Merrill, 1969.

——. *Kant: A Collection of Critical Essays.* Garden City: Doubleday, 1967.

Wood, Allen W. *Kant's Moral Religion.* Ithaca: Cornell University Press, 1970.

INDEX

Absolute value of human beings: and the second formulation of the categorical imperative, 4, 68; as related to Kant's principle of personality, 8, 127; and the categorical imperative, 16, 147; and the good will, 18; as rational agents, 18; and treating persons as mere means, 77, 100, 130, 141, 145, 146; and the end-in-itself, 92, 128, 130, 131, 135, 138, 139, 148; and utilitarianism, 148, 149, 151
Atwell, John E., 101*n*
Autonomy: and the second formulation of the categorical imperative, 4; and moral law, 9, 51, 56, 57, 62, 63, 73, 75, 131; and man as the end-in-himself, 22, 54, 61, 76, 81, 82, 134; and sharing ends, 49, 51, 59, 60; and the will, 51, 52, 53, 54, 56, 59; and Wille, 52, 53, 58, 78, 86, 87, 94, 95, 98, 133, 142; and objective ends, 59, 60, 61, 63; and treating persons as mere means, 83, 100, 126; and duty, 84; and human dignity, 129, 130, 131, 134, 141; and freedom, 134, 135, 141, 142

Bayles, Michael, 125*n*
Beck, Lewis White, 52*n*, 58*n*, 133*n*, 134, 135, 142*n*

Categorical imperatives: and moral-

ity, 10; unconditionality of, 10, 11; and absolute worth of persons, 16; and duty, 73; as opposed to hypothetical imperatives, 109, 138, 139, 142, 146, 147, 149
Content of moral law. *See* Matter of moral law

Dignity, human: and the second formulation of the categorical imperative, 3, 68; as unconditioned worth, 18; test of, 22; and rationality, 23, 25; and Haezrahi, 24; and Kant's theory of morality, 102; and moral worth, 127, 128, 136; and absolute value, 130, 151; and the dignity of virtue, 132; and Willkür, 134; and price, 135, 137, 138, 140, 142; and independence, 141; and being an end-in-oneself, 148
Duty: and respect, 64; and moral worth, 72; and morally right action, 72, 80; and the categorical imperative, 73; and man as an end-in-himself, 83, 84, 86, 87, 88, 122, 123, 125; perfect and imperfect, 110, 112, 113, 115; and moral perfection, 111, 114; and others' happiness, 118, 119, 123, 149; and dignity, 132, 134

Ebbinghaus, Julius, 122*n*
End: standard uses of, 4, 19; man as an, 5, 6, 7; of morality, 11

159

114, 134, 135, 136, 138; and
means, 8; and the categorical imperative, 13; and principle of humanity, 15, 25, 46, 68, 80, 90,
101, 118; and suicide, 30, 31; and
sharing ends, 32–38, 41, 48, 69,
70, 71; as an arbitrary end, 66;
and principle of universality, 78;
and respect, 83, 96, 102; and rational will, 97, 98, 99; and duty,
106, 107, 110, 112, 113, 114, 115,
116, 117, 119; and utilitarianism,
125, 126, 147, 151; and dignity,
128, 129, 143, 151; and hypothetical imperatives, 144, 145
Mill, John Stuart, 20, 20n
Moral law: and man, 10; and God,
10; as holy, 50, 51, 57, 62; and
Wille, 52, 133; and autonomy,
59, 62, 63, 73, 75, 81, 131; and
respect, 66, 114, 116; and man as
an end-in-himself, 91, 107, 127;
and duty, 104, 113, 114, 118, 124;
and moral perfection, 108; and
dignity, 132
Moral rightness: nature of, 72; as
opposed to moral worth, 72, 74,
77; and the categorical imperative, 73
Moral worth: characteristics of, 72;
as opposed to moral rightness,
72, 74, 77
Motives: and duty, 72; and moral
rightness, 73, 80; and moral
worth, 74

Nature of man: as rational, 9, 10,
13, 20, 26; as sensible, 9, 10, 14,
26, 54; as moral, 26

Objective ends: and principle of humanity, 4, 15; and moral law, 6,
105; two kinds of, 7; and categorical imperatives, 11; as opposed to
subjective ends, 11, 12; as applying equally to all human beings,
12; and absolute value, 18; as
positive objective ends, 20; and
Wille, 52, 90
—negative objective ends: as supreme limiting conditions, 12, 61,
81, 92, 96, 105, 106; and the principle of humanity, 15; and man
as an end-in-himself, 50, 88, 91
—positive objective ends: as aims
of everyone's action, 14; and the
principle of humanity, 15, 61; as
opposed to negative objective
ends, 92; and man as an end-in-
himself, 106
Objective principles, 14

Paton, H. J., 29, 29n, 49n, 57, 57n,
58, 66, 66n, 67, 99n, 136, 146n
Perfection, one's own: as duty, 8,
105–7, 110, 111, 112, 113, 114,
116, 117, 118, 123; and sensibility, 10; as objective end, 19n; as
basic end, 69; and development,
108, 109; natural and moral, 108,
115; as intrinsically valuable,
129, 130
Perfection for God: as necessary
feature, 16
Positive concept of man as an end:
and man as an end-in-himself, 7,
8, 18, 107; and as mere means, 8;
and object of will, 69; and principle of humanity, 113
Principle of humanity: Kant's formulation of, 3, 15; as objective
principle, 21; and man as an end-
in-himself, 25, 26, 54, 63, 79, 83,
85, 91, 110, 114; application of,
27, 44, 48; and treating a person
merely as a means, 32, 54, 80, 98,
99, 100, 101; and the content of
morality, 69, 90, 91; and motives,
74; and respect, 75; and principle
of universality, 77, 94. See also
Second formulation of categorical imperative